ADVANCED
SELF DEFENCE

ADVANCED SELF DEFENCE

An Official MAC book

Brian Eustace & David Mitchell

Stanley Paul

London   Melbourne   Auckland   Johannesburg

Stanley Paul & Co. Ltd

An imprint of Century Hutchinson Ltd

62–65 Chandos Place, London WC2N 4NW

Century Hutchinson Australia (Pty) Ltd
PO Box 496, 16–22 Church Street,
Hawthorn, Melbourne, Victoria 3122

Century Hutchinson New Zealand Limited
PO Box 40–086, Glenfield, Auckland 10

Century Hutchinson South Africa (Pty) Ltd
PO Box 337, Bergvlei 2012, South Africa

First published 1988

© Brian Eustace and David Mitchell 1988

This edition: © The Bowerdean Press Ltd.
London EC1

Set in Cheltenham Book by
TJB Photosetting Ltd., South Witham,
Lincolnshire

Printed and bound in Great Britain by
Richard Clay Ltd., Chichester, Sussex

British Library Cataloguing in Publication
Data
Eustace, Brian
     Advanced self defence : an official MAC
     book.
     1. Self-defence
     I. Title   II. Mitchell, David, *1944*–
     613.6'6   GV1111

     ISBN 0–09–172709–X

All photographs by Mike O'Neill

Contents

Foreword

Self defence – The Rationale

This section is a summary which sets out to explain the rationale behind the development of *Advanced Self Defence*. The concept for this originated from the authors, Brian Eustace and David Mitchell where the former contributed the bulk of the practical system and the latter produced the theory.

Now we know that self defence is a way of avoiding a situation where there is a risk of actual attack by one or more assailants. Therefore the best self defence system is one which follows sound principles of observation and evaluation. It is much better to avoid trouble in the first place than to learn how to deal with it once you have walked into it. Any kind of physical response is unsatisfactory and should be regarded as a last resort.

When considering what the course should contain, we had to consider the amount of time most people would be able to commit to it against depth of coverage and effectiveness of certain techniques. We opted for the present course as being a not unreasonable compromise.

Our main source for practical techniques came from the Police Self Defence System which is taught by Home Office approved instructors to the police forces of the United Kingdom but excluding the Metropolitan Force. We chose this source because the police must know how to go into areas of trouble and be able to defend themselves. Their courses are effective, professional and taught within a limited time.

We also went to leading martial artists for their advice on how to improve the basic techniques of the course. For instance, through discussion with Robert Clark, the national coach of the British Jiu Jitsu Association, we identified the circular block as a more sophisticated replacement for the cross block which we originally intended to include.

We found much martial art practice encouraged self defence

techniques which bore little relation to any likely threat. These gave rise to often spectacular responses albeit of little practical value. The techniques we sought would work in response to real attacks, each having the widest possible application. What we didn't want was a technique that would work on one side – the left or the right – but not on both sides.

In a real self defence situation, with all its implied and actual danger, we didn't feel that the average student of less than five years' practice would be able to make an unconscious technique selection. The least techniques we could include, the better.

We therefore worked upon the principle of using a standard response pattern for all types of attack. This principle had to work for a wide variety of ages, sizes and shapes.

Whilst studying the self defence courses originated by others we discovered that there was neither rhyme nor reason to the course content. There was no infrastructure to aid rapid learning. Students learned an array of responses, each requiring a different posture, stance and guard. We felt that though some of these techniques were excellent, they could not be learned within the time-frame of the sort of course we were proposing. We therefore followed the police system in setting out a modular plan.

Our techniques are aggregated into logical sets, the content of which can soon be deduced by the aware student. They progress through the syllabus, becoming gradually more complicated. The mechanics of each technique are learned early on and the rest of the course is intended to build proficiency rather than describe new techniques right up to the last lesson.

Another advantage of this type of modular system is that if you miss training for one reason or another, you can quickly catch up as the cycle of training returns to the point at which you lost contact. This is particularly useful to shift workers.

We have tried to counsel the attacking and defending partners throughout the course. The object of this is to avoid the unwarranted self-confidence that can spring from the deceptively easy rebuttal of pseudo-attacks. We suggest that you try to approximate reality as closely as possible, even to the extent of wearing everyday – albeit old – clothes. Specialised training tunics allow too great a freedom of movement.

Despite all the safeguards, we did consider the possibilities of injury and we advise all persons wishing to practise to spend a few pounds buying the Martial Arts Commission's self defence insurance policy. The address of the Commission is given at the beginning of Chapter 3. This insurance not only provides an injury compensation weekly benefit and capital sums for more serious injuries, it also covers a member-to-member situation. We consider this sort of insurance VITAL to your training.

The Advanced Self Defence Course consists of the following:
1. A theoretical approach to self defence in terms of observation, avoidance, security measures, mental attitude and legal implications.

2. A basic practical approach which looks at exercising, posture, distancing, line, body weapons, force, vulnerable targets and blocks.

3. An advanced practical using a modular system to deal with realistic attacks through an ascending series of techniques.

Referring firstly to the theoretical section, we have tried to teach the student how to use powers of observation to get an early insight into areas of potential danger – a sort of 'early warning' system. This is intended to operate in the same way that other everyday unconscious actions do. You don't think through the precise muscular coordination involved in opening a door every time you do so and there is no need to think specifically about observation. With a little training it will come naturally.

Personal security is important and we have spent some time indicating ways of making your home, car and person more secure. We have suggested ways of responding to various attack situations in the home, on public transport etc.

With observation, evaluation and a sense of security comes the practical application of those principles. Where to sit on a bus and train. How to respond to a possible intruder in the house etc.

The section on law will explain the limits to which you can go in defending yourself. Exceed them and it might be you facing criminal charges – not the burglar! The techniques we have suggested use the minimum of violence conducive to defeating the attacker. It is interesting to note that police officers are constrained to use only the self defence techniques they are taught. This is because the system used is the only one approved by the Home Office. The bobby who takes up karate and kicks someone in the ear will find himself prosecuted and the Home Office refusing to stand behind him.

The physical demands of self defence training are covered in a comprehensive exercise section including the all-important warm-up and cool-down sequences which begin and conclude each training session. By varying the ratio of exercise sets, you will be able to make good any deficiencies of suppleness or fitness and by this means, your training will become more enjoyable and exhilarating.

In terms of the basic practical section, timing means knowing when to respond to an attack and conversely, when not to. There are those self defence situations where a practical response is impossible. In such cases, the best thing to do is wait for an opportunity.

Since techniques are normally aimed at a target, if that target is moved away, or to the side, the attack will miss. This is the concept of distancing and evasion – the two go hand in hand. Often a surprisingly small movement is all that is required to make a technique miss completely. The practical will indicate how you move by the smallest amount in the right direction, leaving time for you to respond without hesitation.

Blocking is a form of insurance which reinforces the evasion mentioned above. A block uses the attacker's force, meeting it obliquely and redirecting it harmlessly away. Performed correctly, this can have spectacular results.

We have explained how to generate force in both striking and leverage techniques. We recommend a relaxed type of technique delivery which does not require a hefty musculature to be effective. We have also mentioned the advantage of short-distance strikes that start close to the target and are difficult to block. In concert with this, we have looked at the vulnerable areas of the opponent's body and suggested ways in which they can be attacked.

We have employed both striking techniques and holds/throws. The former are quicker to learn and the latter more controllable. The principles of leverage ensure that even a small person can subdue a larger opponent but because this class of technique is intrinsically more complex than a strike, they are more difficult to apply. Therefore we have suggested using a strike as an opening distraction to gain time in which to apply the hold/throw.

In linking these techniques, we have been mindful of the attacker's likely response throughout. If that response is unfavourable, the counter-attack can be aborted or changed to another tack.

We considered the usage of these techniques in three situations – the first when the attacker is kept at a safe distance, the second when despite your efforts he has closed and the third when he has actually managed to seize hold of you. Each requires a different approach. The course also contains a section on ground-work. We consider this very important because nearly all self defence situations end up with one or both parties on the ground. You must be able to think and act decisively in a prone as well as an upright position.

We decided to deal with the controversial question of weapons and have based our work with the baton and staff on the police system. We know this works in practice and since it involves relatively simple techniques it is suitable for inclusion within the course framework. We have included a reference to free sparring. We regard this as both instructive and enjoyable and so have set down some general guidelines to assist your practice.

We greatly enjoyed devising this system and hope it will be a positive help to you.

Brian Eustace
David Mitchell   *July 1987*

An Introduction to Self Defence

Self defence is not unarmed combat, though it may contain elements of the latter's repertoire. 'Unarmed combat' is a form of fighting wherein the user has no weapons other than those of the body. It is taught to the Armed Services and is offensive as well as defensive.

Self defence is not martial art, though again it may contain martial art techniques. 'Martial arts' are the techniques of military warfare – both traditional and present-day. They include such things as weapons training and unarmed combat. Over the years, some martial arts have changed to combat sports, or methods of self-discipline through hard training.

What then is 'Self Defence'? A working definition might be 'an action, or series of actions which serve to protect the user(s) from actual or implied violence'.

Self defence is not necessarily a form of fighting and its most sophisticated applications do not use violence at all! This is not a new concept. Consider the story of a famous swordsman in Japan's feudal past. He was sitting quietly in a ferry with a lot of other folk when a drunken samurai got on board. The latter behaved offensively and was making a thorough nuisance of himself so the swordsman asked him to please behave. This enraged the samurai who demanded "What school (of swordfighting) are you from that you dare to speak to me in that manner?"

The swordsman quietly replied, "I am from the no-hands school; I do not even have to use my hands to win a duel."

There and then the samurai demanded satisfaction but the swordsman replied, "Not on this crowded boat. It would be best to duel on yonder island." He indicated a small island in midstream that the boat was fast approaching. As the boat hove to, the samurai leapt off and drew his sword. The swordsman on the other hand, bade the oarsmen to cast off and left the samurai fuming behind.

The swordsman called back, "That is how we defeat opponents in the 'no hands' school!"

Self defence is knowing how to minimise the risk of violence by using observation, commonsense, assertiveness (where it will benefit the situation), escape, and when all else fails, a small number of practical techniques.

We make no claims about these practical techniques. Their value to you personally will depend upon many things. If you are naturally timid, then at least you will have learned some practical self defence techniques. Not that there is anything wrong in being timid! People who are aware of their own limitations are the least likely to get into situations where a physical response is necessary. Just as long as your ego will allow you to tolerate someone kicking sand in your face!

Many self defence teachers have no real knowledge about the widespread application of their techniques in an actual self defence situation. We believe that those we suggest do work because they rely heavily upon the substantial knowledge and expertise of Britain's police forces. They regularly encounter situations of actual attack, not like the scenarios imagined by others.

The techniques selected use the minimum of force, so you are less likely to face a G.B.H. charge through defending yourself too enthusiastically. The system offers a series of different response levels, from low intensity and discreet 'hands off!' up to full-blooded throws and holds.

Even the most effective techniques demand little in the way of body conditioning, unlike those old traditional martial art schools where students were obliged to spend years smashing their knuckles into straw pads. Quite respectable results can be obtained by attacking vulnerable points on the opponent's body with relatively simple impact techniques. A surprising amount of discomfort can be inflicted by a person of average strength operating the principles of leverage. This simplicity however is that which comes from sophistication rather than the simplicity of low-level techniques.

The system is a mix of impact with grappling techniques, such that the more quickly learned strikes provide an initial if limited cover, whilst the more complex holds and throws contribute at a later stage. Furthermore both have been fitted into a teaching system that is easier to learn than the haphazard collection of unrelated self defence techniques offered by many teachers.

You will see that the practical part of the course is arranged into a series of modules so that groups of movements rather than individual techniques are taught. This is because we want you to grasp the whole response, to think in terms of one movement, and this approach would not be served by chopping everything up into small sections.

The techniques can be studied at home though we would advise joining a club, or training with a group of friends. A third-party can often see what is wrong with the way you are trying to do a technique and put you right before that error becomes ingrained.

Those of you who are young and fit to stand to gain the most benefit from training but even if you aren't as fast as you used to be, you will still gain something from your practice. We would not wish to make any claims about how proficient you will become because that is purely a matter for you. Your determination to defend yourself effectively counts for more than your present age, sex and health. Having said that, don't be over-confident!

We designed the course to run for around 50 lessons, each of 90 minutes duration. Some of you will learn quickly, others slowly but by the end of the course, you will all know that much more about self defence. A shorter course would have meant fewer techniques with reduced scope whilst on the other hand, you may not have the time commitment for a longer one.

At the end of your course you may feel like doing some further training. At the moment the only possibility is to join a martial arts club recognised by the Martial Arts Commission and we have provided some further information on that route in Chapter 3. However, we do not rule out the development of further courses and by keeping in touch with the Martial Arts Commission you will know when these are due to begin.

1

Self Defence & The Law

The law can be a bit unkind to the successful self defence student insofar as if you defend yourself with too much zeal, it could well be you who is prosecuted. Therefore you would do well to realise at the outset that not only the victim but the attacker too has rights in law.

Bear in mind that you may only use 'reasonable' force in beating off attack and what is reasonable will vary according to the circumstances. Whatever you do may well be analysed sometime afterwards in the intellectual arena of the courtroom.

If for example, you are a large martial artist, your response must cause the attacker minimum harm because as every court knows, there is only one class of martial artist and that is the expert. Such an expert is wrongly seen as always being able to select and use a suitable minimum-violence response, even in a fraught situation. To a lesser extent, the same is true for people who are known to have practised judo, boxing or wrestling.

In fact it is only those people who habitually face and deal with actual (rather than feigned) violence who may retain sufficient composure to react in a sensible manner. For most of us – even trained martial artists – the threat of violence is unnerving and our response accordingly less controlled.

The threshold of reasonability is substantially raised for non-martial artists but even then it will depend upon the size and shape of the victim. As with the martial artist victim, this criterion is unfair because it wrongly presupposes that a large person automatically behaves less emotionally and with more control than a small one.

The threshold is raised to another order when the victim is a small person facing large odds.

If someone attacks you with a chainsaw, then you may well be excused for responding violently because clearly you are facing grave personal peril. Will the court accept that you were facing a similar level of danger when you stabbed a younger, smaller and unarmed attacker to death with a kitchen knife? The violent sixteen year old would-be attacker may present a totally different picture when he comes to court in his school uniform, sporting the injuries you have inflicted whilst fending him off.

If there is any chance that you are facing more than the possibility of slight physical damage, then we would advise you to react in a way you consider appropriate, remove your person from danger and worry about the legal consequences afterwards.

Recent psychological studies of attackers reveal that few are motivated towards violence because they have no money for food or shelter. In many cases they are opportunists who see a chance to benefit in some way. Drug addicts are driven by compulsions beyond their ability to control and may attempt violence as a means of obtaining money for their next fix. These are best dealt with by giving them the money.

The majority of attackers think only of themselves and their selfish desires, and cannot feel for others. It is this indifference that must be broken down if the attacker is to be deterred by non-violent means. Try to reason with the attacker; ask him what his mother/sister would think if someone did it to them. Speak in as calm a voice as you can muster and avoid showing signs of alarm and fear which so often act as fuel for violence.

If this tack fails and it is impossible to run away, then a physical response may be required. If this succeeds and the attacker is distracted, use the time available to run away. Don't haul off and kick him into insensibility, or seize a milk bottle and bring it violently down onto his lowered head. If you disarm your attacker, threaten him with the weapon but don't just stick it in him. If you have taken up a knife and feel you must use it, then try only to injure his extremities and avoid attacking the face or trunk. Do not take up a weapon unless you are capable of using it and if you are not, throw it out of harm's way.

Do not carry a long hatpin, or a paper-topped pot containing pepper. Avoid also the little daggers that conceal in key rings and belt buckles. These can be construed by the police as offensive weapons and their possession is an offence for which you can be prosecuted. Moreover, possessing a weapon may well give you a sense of false confidence so you overlook the elementary principles of observation and perhaps walk into a position where you are obliged to use your weapon.

In all cases we consider that the best way of dealing with any threat of violence is to see whether it is possible to avoid the need for a physical response. If money is all that is at stake, then let it go. The loss of £50 is of much less importance than the risk of a disfigured face.

The important thing is to use your common sense and avoiding a high risk situation will obviate the need for a practical self defence response and keep you on the right side of the law.

2

The Martial Arts and Self Defence

Self defence is generally associated with the practice of what are commonly called the martial arts and this section will explore that linkage and use it to open further avenues of study.

The term 'martial arts' is widely misused to encompass a range of fighting systems originating in the Far Eastern countries of China, Korea, Japan, Malaysia and Thailand. Some are combat sports, others claim to be methods for improving the character and a minority were once used by the armed forces of a nation and can therefore legitimately describe themselves as 'martial arts'.

Be that as it may, nearly all of them involve some form of combat between participants. This combat is rigorously inhibited by rules designed to improve safety and though often violent, it is nevertheless far removed from the self defence situations encountered today.

No martial arts practised today and regarded by their followers as 'effective' can truly claim to be based upon the needs of modern street self defence. Arguably the most modern is at least thirty years out of date, if not more. Most were built upon a system originally designed around armed soldiers with the unarmed section playing only a small part. Despite that, in many cases it has nowadays come to represent the whole martial art.

The traditional martial artist tries to practise a system exactly as he or she imagines it was practised when all further development had halted. Indeed attempts to introduce new thinking into such systems often provoke a fierce rejection.

Some leading martial artists decided to introduce an element of philosophy into their obsolete martial art and changed it according to this realignment. Such changes are most clearly seen in Japanese martial arts and can be recognised by the presence of the suffix *do* (pronounced 'doe') in their titles. Thus *Karate-do* is a system based upon the original fighting techniques of Okinawan Karate. *Aiki-do* is based upon a part of the Japanese warrior's fighting system previously known as *Aiki – Jiujitsu*.

Each of these systems contains techniques and applications which can be applied to modern day self defence though they must be sieved out from the welter of ritual and unusable material. Who is to say what is an effective technique for a self defence situation? Can the instructor of a martial arts club tell you? How would he know? Has he regularly applied his techniques in a true self defence situation? Has he proof that they work for a wide cross-section of the class? These are questions which need to be answered before anyone can set themselves up as an expert on self defence.

Even expert martial artists are confused over the criteria for deciding if a particular martial art technique is suitable for self defence. Identification is made difficult because in the ordered cooperation of the martial art training hall, all techniques seem to work effectively, if not even spectacularly. But what would happen if the opponent did not move in precisely the way expected? You can find that out for yourself by watching the beginners practising.

Given that a technique can accommodate a margin of error on both sides and actually works, can it be learned in a relatively short time? Those best able to show the effectiveness of a technique are the advanced students – people who have spent several years practising. It is no use marvelling at the effectiveness of a particular technique only to discover that its application in a realistic self defence situation is well-nigh impossible for anyone with less than 20 years experience of it.

The way in which some martial arts teach techniques militates against their early usefulness for self defence. To accommodate large classes, sequences of movement were broken into single techniques. Students were taught to first block the punch and then respond to it, so the response was thought of as a two stage process. Whilst the reasons for doing this can be understood, it is nevertheless bad practice for any feasible system of self defence. An effective system of techniques must be taught and learned as a unit right from the start, so when the time comes to use it, it will be reproduced in that form.

By now you will appreciate that studying martial arts, judo, boxing or wrestling will not automatically make you into a skilled self defender. It is however likely that a prolonged study will make you better able to defend yourself.

Having viewed martial arts from the perspective of self defence, let us now examine the principal forms in more detail. Please note that there is no such thing as a 'best' martial art, though there may be one best suited to your age, temperament and physique.

What follows is a short introduction to a number of martial arts. If you would like to take up one of them, contact the Martial Arts Commission from the details given in the next chapter.

Aikido

Aikido is a Japanese system based upon an older martial art. It uses leverage against limb joints, allowing a skilled practitioner to defeat a larger opponent. The system is based upon the principle of non-direct response; that is to say it does not meet the opponent's force head on in a contest of strength but rather tries to use that force against the attacker. This is best seen in displays of pure aikido but is less evident when the art is used in a sporting or self defence context.

Full Contact

Full contact is a Western originated combat sport using techniques taken from boxing and other fighting systems. It is best thought of as boxing plus kicks, and its nearest relatives are Thai Boxing and La Savate. Full contact competitions are savage affairs with no pulled blows. Knockouts are far from uncommon. Full contact training does not necessarily involve competition and consequently it can be practised by agile and powerful persons. Being a system based only on striking, its techniques are quickly learned.

Hapkido

Hapkido is a Korean system containing a mixture of striking techniques similar to those of Taekwondo and Tang Soo Do, with limb-leverage techniques like those of Aikido. This similarity of technique is only to be expected because there are a limited number of ways in which the hands and feet can be used as offensive weapons. Hapkido seems in many ways to have the best of both worlds in that the striking techniques (which are taught first) are quickly learned whilst the grappling techniques come later and are as effective as those of aikido. The only other system with a similar spread of technique is Shorinji Kempo.

Jiu-Jitsu

Jiu jitsu is a Japanese martial art deriving from part of the samurai's syllabus. It is a mixed system of grappling and striking techniques though the former are more developed. It claims one of the largest syllabuses of any system and there is an ongoing development of techniques to bring them into line with modern day situations. Like Aikido, the principles of Jiu jitsu lie in harmonising with the attacker's strength though this is not easily seen in the modern schools. In response to an attack, the typical Jiu jitsu response is to block or evade, distract the opponent with a painful strike to a vulnerable target and then apply a painful immobilising hold. A throw is often interposed between the strike and the hold.

Karate
Karate is a Japanese developed system which originally trained the hands and feet to be used as weapons. It is almost entirely a pure striking system and uses the scientific application of physical principles to increase the power of its impacts. Because it is a striking system, it is more quickly learned than those based upon grappling though it may not be as versatile. Some styles of karate have become competition orientated and this may well have a detrimental effect upon their self defence potential.

Kendo
This is a Japanese system using bamboo practice swords and armour. At first glance it might appear to have no self defence value whatsoever. Having said that, the vigorous sparring teaches coordination and tactics which can be extrapolated to self defence.

Kung fu
Kung fu is the commonly used term for a whole range of Chinese systems. Some of these use weapons and others do not. 'External' systems rely on physical strength and speed whilst 'internal' forms place emphasis on less obvious factors. As if this weren't complicated enough, the same system can be practised differently depending upon whether it comes from the 'Northern' or 'Southern' schools. Add to this several hundred variants of each, practised by individual 'families' and small schools! One of the simplest and most quickly learned systems is called *Wing chun*. This is a close range and effective fighting system based upon striking techniques.

Shorinji Kempo
This is a Japanese system claiming descent from a classical Chinese Kung fu school associated with the Buddhist temple of Shaolin. Like Hapkido it is a mix of striking and grappling techniques and many of the same comments apply to both. It is also the vehicle for the promulgation of a form of Buddhism.

Taekwondo
Taekwondo is the name given to a Korean system using kicks,

punches and strikes. It employs a great many high kicks and is therefore seen at its best in people who have trained from an early age. It tests the power of its techniques by breaking wooden boards with them. There is a well developed international competition structure and protective equipment is worn to mitigate the effects of the powerful techniques used.

Tang Soo Do

This is also a Korean system of kicks and punches but is less combat sport orientated.

Thai Boxing

As its name implies, Thai Boxing is a combat sport and like Full contact, competition uses full power attacks to the face and head.

3

The Martial Arts Commission

Though you may know very little about self defence, there is nothing to prevent you from opening a school and setting yourself up as its teacher. For spurious authenticity, you can copy part of a Chinese take-away menu and get your local printer to run you up an imposing looking certificate of competence. Don't laugh because there are not a few self defence teachers who have done precisely that.

To be sure, some have studied martial arts such as karate and kung fu for a time, though whether they ever became any good as a result is open to conjecture. Even more worrying, there are associations of martial artists which for a remuneration, will affiliate you as an accredited teacher of a chosen discipline. In 1986, one such association sent a teaching diploma to an alsatian dog and another sent a certificate of high grade to a Chinese waiter with no martial arts experience!

You cannot rely upon newspaper references, you cannot count on certificates, so what can you depend upon for a reference? The sole answer is the Martial Arts Commission, or 'MAC'. MAC has been in existence for ten years. It was set up by Britain's responsible martial artists who were perturbed enough about the situation to band together and set standards for practice. The MAC's two main objectives are to enhance the technical standards of martial arts and self defence practice whilst concurrently encouraging a spirit of social responsibility amongst its membership.

The Martial Arts Commission ensures that its registered coaches have a high enough skill level to be able to teach you valid techniques. Furthermore its coach training schemes mean that your self defence instructor can pass on his/her skills with efficiency and safety.

There is an additional good reason for training only in an MAC-recognised club and that is the insurance available to MAC licenceholders. There are now over 100,000 MAC licensed practitioners and this represents substantial purchasing power from the point of view of insurance. Your membership of the MAC includes a personal accident and public liability policy which not only provides weekly and capital benefits in the unlikely event of injury but also indemnifies you against claims arising if you inadvertently injure your training partner.

Because your self defence coach is registered with the MAC, he/she will most likely have a professional indemnity policy to cover them against claims arising out of accidents occurring during practice.

The Martial Arts Commission is the only governing body for the martial arts and self defence in membership of the prestigious Central Council for Physical Recreation. Additionally the MAC receives grand aid from the Sports Council to regulate and control practice for the safety of the public.

So when you decide to join a reputable self defence club, remember to contact the Martial Arts Commission on 01–691–3433, or write to them at 1st Floor Broadway House, 15–16 Deptford Broadway, London SE8 4PE.

You won't be sorry you did!

The First Line of Self Defence

The first line of self defence is perhaps the most important – learn to recognise situations of potential danger and avoid them. Curiously it seems that those least likely to suffer assault and battery are old age pensioners and women – not because they are poor targets but because they are aware of the real danger that exists and take steps to minimise it. Younger people do not appear to be so aware.

As a general rule, do realise that darkness provides cover and those places which are relatively safe during daylight hours may not be once the light has gone. A powerful torch is useful in such instances because it can dazzle a would-be attacker, gaining you precious seconds in which to react. The best torches for this purpose are those with xenon bulbs powered by alkaline penlight batteries. They are made from a light but strong aluminium alloy that can stand a sharp impact.

Remember also that the attacker shuns attention and if you shout or scream loudly and persistently, you may succeed in driving him off. There are anti-theft sound alarms which emit a deafening scream when activated. These may be effective in such cases.

If you are carrying valuables, split them up and don't have them all in one bag or pocket; that way you won't lose everything if you are robbed. Keep a note of your credit card numbers so you can cancel them immediately if your wallet is stolen. Do this NOW!

Let's begin by looking at how we can be less susceptible to attack. First of all ensure your house is secure by fitting mortice locks to all external doors. These must be recessed into enough wood to withstand heavy impacts. This may involve reinforcing the door and frame. Do not leave keys in the locks or a hand can be inserted through a broken pane of door glass and your secure door easily opened.

Your external doors should preferably be made from solid wood without glass panels. Get a good look at the caller by means of a spy-viewer that gives a fish-eye view. Have a working porch light and install a panic alarm switch somewhere near the front door. This is tamper-proof and sets off a siren or bell when activated. The de-activating key should be hidden somewhere else in the house and not left in the unit.

A security chain strongly screwed into substantial woodwork allows you to open the door far enough to take in identification cards, telephone directories or parcels. Whilst it will not stop a determined intruder, it will buy enough time for you to activate the panic alarm and escape to another room with a lockable door.

Keep all your external doors locked and let no-one in until you have established who they are. All gas and electricity officials have identification cards and you should examine these closely before allowing entry. This is especially important if there is more than one caller because whilst one is engaging you in conversation, the other might be rifling through your belongings.

Fit latch locks to all opening windows and never assume any one is too small to allow entry. French windows need a strong security lock.

Don't leave any ladders in the garden or in an easily burgled shed because these can be used to effect entry at bedroom level.

If someone does succeed in gaining entry, leave as quickly as you can and run to a neighbour's house. On no account try to tackle an intruder. If you are upstairs and it is night time, turn on all the lights and make as much noise as you can. Call out as though to another occupant but don't call "Who's there?" or otherwise tip the intruder off that you're alone in the house.

If you can safely escape from an upstairs window then by all means do so. Otherwise collect any children quickly and without fuss, taking them all into one bedroom and barricading the door. Door wedges are inexpensive items but when properly inserted, they prevent a door from opening short of it being totally destroyed. Whilst this is happening, you can be telephoning for help or shouting out of the window.

Don't make it easy for the intruder to catch you as you escape or summon help. Upset chairs or tables in his path, pull doors shut, or throw things in his way such as chairs, boxes, crockery, milk bottles etc. If you take up a weapon as a deterrent, be prepared to use it – otherwise leave it where it is. When selecting a weapon, choose one that looks the part and which can be managed in the space available. If the intruder is armed, pick up anything you can use to shield yourself. Is there anything you can throw at him such as an iron, kettle of boiling water or heavy crockery?

When driving your car, try to avoid pulling up next to a crowd of disorderly people. Hang back or drive on past them. Don't allow yourself to be halted but drive firmly through them, even though the car may collect a dent or two. Keep your doors locked and windows rolled up tightly and report the incident to the nearest police station as soon as you can. If you are forced to a stop, or stall the car and come under attack, sound your horn loudly and continuously. Avoid driving with windows down in potentially hazardous areas of the city.

If you are in a car park and strangers approach, do not be intimidated into offering a lift. Decide whether you have time to get into the car and lock it before they get close and if not, leave the car locked and make off in the opposite direction. Always approach the car with your ignition keys in your hand so as to save time rummaging through pockets or bag. Be prepared to leave groceries outside as you close and lock your doors in the face of danger.

You can never be sure whether an attacker will be content to simply take your car. He may well produce a knife and take you with him to somewhere more secluded. Therefore don't imagine that by offering your car keys you will be able to escape.

If you are on a bicycle, cycle quickly away from potential hazards and if a car follows you, try and nip down into pedestrian precincts. Alternatively make a sharp u-turn and ride off in the opposite direction. Make use of the bicycle's manoeuverability to avoid being trapped.

Don't sit on the upper deck of buses at night, even if you are a smoker. Sit downstairs near the driver or exit doors so you can either summon help or get off quickly to avoid trouble. Don't wait for your bus at a dark and deserted bus stop but choose instead a well lit road with lots of traffic passing. When travelling by train, choose a railway carriage where there are people of both sexes and change compartments rather than sit alone in an empty one.

If you have been to a party, take some inconspicuous clothes with you to wear on the journey home. Don't have too much to drink or you may find yourself missing danger signals and getting into a predicament. Make sure you know the person offering you a lift home, otherwise decline and get a cab. If you are going back by public transport, telephone home and let them know what time you expect to arrive. Perhaps a friend or relation can meet you at the station or bus stop.

Avoid walking towards noisy and aggressive gangs of men. Cross the road rather than to walk past them. Do not respond to any remarks or behaviour, keep your head up and your gaze steady. Try not to look frightened or intimidated.

Avoid poorly lit short-cuts when walking at night and always stay on busy roads even if it means going the long way round. If you cannot avoid walking along a deserted street, keep in the outer third of the pavement where you can see into shop doorways and alleys. If you're not sure about them, move into the road and give them a wide berth. As you walk along, constantly note the houses with lights on, so you can run to one without delay should the need arise.

Waste ground and parklands are particularly dangerous at night because they are poorly lit and there are many places for concealment. Plan your route so you give them a wide detour.

If you hear footsteps behind you, gradually increase the length of your stride and cross the road. This will give you a chance to see who is walking along behind. Try not to break into a run unless you are convinced you are being stalked and then run only to someone's front door or back out onto a main road.

Decline any offers of lifts and remain out of grabbing distance of kerb-crawlers. Make a play of noting the number of any persistent crawlers and quickly double back and retrace your footsteps.

5

Make a Poor Target

Unless the would-be attacker is insane, or suffering acute drug withdrawal symptoms, he will select his victim according to two fundamental criteria. First of all, the victim must be in the right place at the right time and secondly he or she must be a suitable target. We covered ways of reducing easy access to a potential victim in the previous chapter and must now consider ways of making the available target less suitable.

Few attackers would consider taking on a 2 metre tall paratrooper with a face marked by an interest in boxing unless they were armed with the kind of weapon that ensures superiority regardless of physical size. The ideal victim is one the attacker identifies as likely to submit to threats or to an opening act of violence and will thereafter comply with demands made without a constant and exhausting struggle.

Large people are threatened as often as small ones when it is obvious to the attacker that they will submit. There is perhaps something in their demeanour that shows they will not put up much of a fight. Maybe they don't lock gazes but look frantically around for an avenue of escape. Their voice becomes higher pitched and they may begin shouting. This indicates the level of panic going on within. The fact that you may be neither nice-looking nor young and nubile no longer appears to be a shield against sexual attack.

Unless there has been a drawn-out confrontation, the victim will at first be paralysed by the thought that 'This isn't happening to me'. The attack is so vicious and without warning that he or she has little time to even be frightened but is locked instead into numbed immobility. Even skilled martial artists can react this way, though afterwards they kick themselves for not using the many techniques at their disposal. 'Why didn't I think of that!' If the attacker gives warning of intent, then there is time for panic to set in and once again a carefully practised response can go by the board.

Actually no self defence course can help you overcome the fear inherent in a situation of attack. The most that can be achieved is to educate you into adopting ways of minimising the risk of it happening. When that fails, repeated training in a limited number of responses may allow you to unconsciously throw out an effective technique perhaps more from desperation than by intent.

All we can do is offer some fairly facile advice on trying to keep as calm as you can. If you are sitting down when the assailant approaches, stand up straight and face them from a safe distance. Carry your hands loose at your sides or grasp them together in front of your lap. Lock gazes with the assailant and turn your head to look full at them. Don't rely on eye movement alone. Try to keep your voice low and firm. Don't plead, argue or threaten but ask what the attacker wants. Try to speak meaningfully and avoid repeating yourself. Make your expression match what you are saying. For example, don't say "No!" whilst looking apologetic. Keep your face as expressionless as you can manage.

Much is said about offering violence against an attacker. Certainly an ineffectual physical response may well excite a certain type of attacker and make you liable to escalated violence but for the motiveless attacks on young men, violence alone seems to be the object and submission is no guarantee whatsoever that you will escape lightly. Having said that, if the attacker merely wants your money then by all means give it up. It is only when you are unsure of what the attacker wants that you should even contemplate a physical response.

Are you capable of responding effectively? When originating our self defence system, we considered many highly effective techniques but discarded them when we discovered that students were squeamish and didn't think they could ever bring themselves to use them. These included such things as attacks to the eyes.

Whatever response you make must be wholehearted and a 100% commitment otherwise it will prove worse than useless. A violent reaction will cause the attacker to reassess his choice of target and given that many are opportunists, you may succeed in discouraging him. Certainly there are many cases where old ladies and small persons fought off younger and potentially more powerful attackers. They did that not because they were martial arts experts or 2 metre tall ex-paratroopers but because they simply refused to go down without a fight.

There are a number of tricks you can use to discourage the attacker – especially if you are female and confirm a sexual motive. You could mention that you are having a period, you suffer from Herpes II, or even carrying the HIV A.I.D.S. virus. There was one case where the victim appeared to acquiesce to her attacker's advances and went willingly into his arms but only to tightly grasp his testicles!

You can also avoid certain kinds of attack by refusing to respond to goading. For those of us with a strong self image this is hard to do – especially if we are male and in female company. Insults against one's partner, especially those of a sexual nature, are very difficult to ignore and the psychological scars of doing so can be long-lasting. However they may be less long lasting than the after-effects of serious physical injury. The sensible would-be victim will remember the quotation 'Discretion is the better part of valour, wherebye I save my life'.

6

Keep on the Right Foot

If someone is likely to punch you any second now and you stand facing them, hands at your side and not more than the length of their arm away, then you deserve to be hit! Yet with some thought and little all else, you can make yourself very difficult to be hit. Consider, for his attack to succeed, you must be close enough for the punch or kick to land, the attack must have a clear flight to the target and the chosen technique be suitable for the target presented.

Instead of facing your opponent with your hands hanging at your sides, stand at an angle of forty-five degrees and keep your feet no more than a shoulder-width apart. Clasp your hands together in front of your thighs if you like (*fig 1*). Turn your head so you are looking directly at your opponent.

1

This is a low-key stance with distinct advantages to standing square-on. First of all it doesn't look aggressive. You are looking directly at the opponent and therefore taking him seriously yet your hands are not raised in any kind of threatening gesture. However, he will not have noticed that you have drawn half of your body back and reduced the target area by half. Moreover you now have one foot closer to him than the other and the effect of this is to close off your groin to all but a turning kick. This is a stance which recognises that you face the possibility of attack. It is called 'Ready stance'.

As soon as the attacker makes an overt threatening move, step back half a pace with your rear foot and bring your hands up. Don't pull them into fists because this indicates a willingness to fight back and there is no sense in providing the attacker with early clues of your intention. If you have your right foot forward, lead with your right hand, turning the palm slightly towards the attacker.

Keep your right arm well out from you body and bend it 90° at the elbow. It should be in the plane of the mid-line of your body. Your left hand is also on the centre line but it is much closer to your

body. Slightly bend your knees – but not so much that it looks as though you are crouching. Concentrate your weight on the balls of your feet. This is an effective defensive stance (*fig 2*) and one from which you can mount your response to attack.

If you look at this stance from the attacker's viewpoint, you can see that large areas of your body are now obscured. Your leading guard hand can either be used for mounting a fast short-distance strike, or it can slap an incoming punch out of the air. Your rear hand acts both as a second line of defence and it can also mount powerful punches. In fact you now have what is called a 'Guard'. The combination of stance and guard seems to be saying, "Look, I don't want trouble," and this is a better message than the one evoked by raised fists.

Don't hold your front hand too high or you will expose your ribs. Maximum is when your fingertips are at shoulder height. Don't hold your leading hand too straight either, or you won't be able either to snap punch or slap block without a tell-tale initial withdrawal. Keep your rear hand in the mid-line because if it is too far across your stomach, or pulled too far back onto the rear hip, you won't be able to use it quickly and effectively.

Don't let your stance lengthen because this reduces agility. There should be no more than a pace and a half distance between the toes of the rear foot and the heel of the leading foot. Don't stand with the feet too close together either because this is unsuitable both for resisting a strong attack and for launching a powerful response.

If you look closely at the way the feet are placed, you will see that the stance has width as well as length to it. In fact the toes of the front foot are in line with the heel of the rear foot, giving the stance an element of lateral stability. Compare this to a stance where the rear foot is well out to the side. This exposes the groin to attack. The converse, with no side-step at all is unstable.

Remember always to keep an effective guard as you move. If you change leading leg, smoothly change your guard too. If you don't, you'll find the reverse hand forwards (*fig 3*) and large parts of your body exposed as potential targets. Spend some time practising moving your guard as you step, so you don't have to consciously think about it.

Most people prefer to deal with others from a distance and feel threatened when there is an unwarranted incursion into this 'personal zone'. Preserving this zone is vital to good self defence because it allows you to keep the attacker at a distance greater

Fig 3

than he can reach without stepping forward. If the attacker has to step forward to reach you, then you have time to respond. If he is close enough to be able to reach you without stepping, then he is simply too close.

If he steps towards you, take a pace back from ready stance to the fully-fledged defensive stance. If he continues to come forwards but more slowly, first step back half a pace with your rear foot and then draw the leading foot back after it. Draw your leading foot back the correct amount to prevent your stance from elongating. If he rushes forwards, take a big step back with the rear foot (*fig 4*), then pull your front foot quickly back so it brushes the rear foot (*fig 5*) and then veers out to the side (*fig 6*).

Fig 4   Fig 5   Fig 6

This is an effective way of both moving back and out of line. The amount by which you step back can be regulated by the distance your rear foot slides and by the size of the back-pace you take with the leading leg. For retreating the shortest distance, don't bother sliding back the rear foot first but simply step backwards in a semicircle . By varying the side-step, you can also alter the amount to which you move out of line.

Use these same methods for advancing too by simply reversing the sequences. For a small advance, slide first the leading foot, then quickly draw up the rear. For a more substantial advance, first slide your front foot forwards – either straight or on the diagonal, then sweep the rear leg up and past in a semicircular step. The zig-zagging movement this produces both covers ground quickly and confuses the attacker.

Fig 7   Fig 8   Fi

Practise also a simple 90° turn by stepping to the outside with your leading leg (*fig 7*) and pivoting on it (*fig 8*). The more side-step you take, the more you move to the side. A 180° turn uses the rear leg. First look behind to see whether it is clear to turn, then step across and past the line of the front foot (*fig 9*), keeping the sliding foot grazing lightly over the ground with heel raised. Pivot around when it has moved an equal distance to the side (*fig 10*).

Step too far across with your rear foot and the turn will open your stance out, exposing the groin to attack. Step too little and your stance will lose that vital side-step component and stability suffers.

Illustration 1

Consider the first diagram (*Illus. 1*) which shows a plan-view of two people facing each other. Note how both are leading with their left legs and each can hit the other with virtually any technique. Compare this with the second diagram (*Illus. 2*) and although both are still in left stance, neither can easily hit the other. Why is that? In the first diagram, each person's leading foot is inside the other's but in the second diagram, both leading feet are virtually in line. This forces the attacker to use only his front hand for a fast attack and even then he must lean well forwards. If he wants to use his rear hand or foot, he has to twist his body around first, providing cues.

Illustration 2

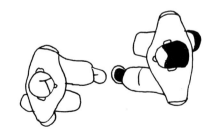

The clever tactician can stand slightly to the outside of the attacker's front foot but turn towards him. This means that though he can't use all his body weapons to attack you, you can

Fig 10

use all yours to attack him. Don't make your step to the side too obvious otherwise he will simply turn to face you and you will lose the advantage.

Always maintain a proper stance, at the correct distance and with the proper line.

If you move towards the attacker, go to the outside of his front foot. Make the movement smooth and don't raise your guard as though to strike him. As you close range, he will respond according to the degree of threat he feels. If he registers cues signalling a hard technique crossing his personal safety zone, he will immediately take evasive action. He may have noticed your sudden dart forward, seen your hand come up and your face contort as you channel your energy, and even though your technique is fast and on target, it may be defeated.

On the other hand, if your advance is smoother and slightly slower, a lower energy strike might well get through because the absence of strong threat cues may not ring alarm bells. Therefore practise moving smoothly and without sudden darting movements. Use lower energy short distance opening techniques for the best chance of success.

Use feints to distract and confuse the attacker. For example, a feint to the attacker's eyes will cause him to blink and look away, providing an opening for your higher energy follow-up technique. A feint snap kick at the groin brings the attacker's head down in a reflex flinch, opening him to a follow-up technique.

For the feint to cause a distraction, it must look like a serious attack in its own right. By all means provide an abundance of cues, since these distract the attacker away from the all-important follow-up. If you make it obvious you are going to try and punch him on the nose, he will pull his face back out of danger and perhaps block. If you have aimed the feint to the side of his face, his blocking hand may momentarily obscure his vision, allowing a second but lower strike to his groin to pass through un-blocked.

For the best results, always widely separate the targets for feint and follow-up. The effect of the feint is very short-lived so make sure your follow-up technique is ready and waiting in the wings. If the feint hasn't worked, don't go through with the follow-up, or you may run on to something nasty. Remember too that the feint may result in masking the secondary target because of the way the attacker reacts.

7

When to Respond to Attack

It is not a good idea to attempt to defend yourself when a knife is being held to your throat. Though this is a fairly extreme example it suffices to describe the essence of when to react and when not to. In any self defence situation there will be circumstances where there is little or no opportunity for you to successfully respond. You must come to know how to recognise these.

People who are shouting are unlikely to attack you. If they are sufficiently emotional to shout, then a soft reply or apology, even if unwarranted will not rouse them more and may succeed in lowering the temperature. Beware the person who speaks in a quieter voice and moves close.

If you think that an attack is certain, then the best form of defence is attack. So don't wait for a punch, kick or grab. A feint followed by a powerful attack may be all you need to escape. If someone is getting out of a car ostensibly to thump you, or to drag you inside, jam him in the door before he's clear and see what targets are available.

If he throws a punch, try and stop it even before it has got moving and counter-attack whilst his mind is fixed on thumping you. Because the technique has only started, it will not have developed full power and so should be easy to cope with. Unless he is a skilful fighter, he will be thinking in terms of a single good shot rather than a fusillade of jolting punches and it will take a little time to call up a replacement.

If you've left it too late and the punch is well on the way, avoid it by jumping back or stepping to the side and even as it misses, close quickly and counter-attack. All powerful techniques need time to recover if they miss and any counter-attack launched during this time will stand a greater chance of catching the attacker on the wrong foot. For this concept to work, it is important that you don't move too far away from the attack. There really is only a split second before recovery is complete and the next technique ready to go.

Mid-way between these two alternatives is a third, that of responding to the technique as it is reaching maximum power. This requires a fair degree of skill because you must identify the technique from body and limb posture and make the correct evasion. Whilst the technique is actually accelerating, there is little the attacker can do to abort it and provided you have fast reactions, a positive and effective counter can be made at this point.

Having discussed the options for launching your counter-attack, we pass on now to the mechanics of evasion. The purpose of evasion is to make an attack fail by moving the target by the minimum amount compatible for safety, in the right direction and out of the path of the attack.

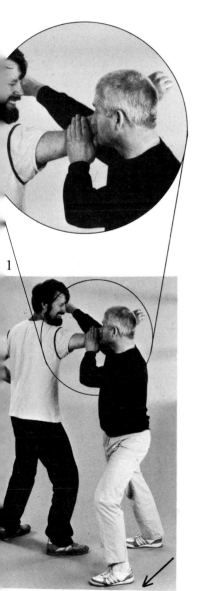

The simplest evasion is the step backwards away from the attack. This will make the majority of attacks miss and as long as you close distance quickly afterwards, you can deliver a counter-attack safely and effectively. Stepping back out of harm's way is very safe because it has taken you outside the range of the incoming attack. However, you must be able to close very quickly to avoid the follow-up technique.

The step back need not be a full pace. If space is restricted, you can simply slide your rear foot back a short distance and bring your body weight back over it. If you do this, keep your face back out of trouble and don't stick your bottom out. You can also step diagonally backwards by taking a short step out and back with the rear foot, then drawing up the front foot and leaning away to make the attack miss.

If you can read the cues for an attack correctly, it is possible to evade by stepping inside the attack. Generally it is safest to do this by moving sideways or diagonally forwards to the attacker's blind side. This makes use of line (discussed in Chapter 6) to render the opponent's techniques ineffective whilst leaving yours with their maximum potential. Be careful not to step into the path of a straight punch!

You can make do with just the plain sidestep of the front foot, using ridge-hand (*fig 11*), snap kick or side thrust kick to counter. Notice how an effective guard protects the face against wild strikes. The sidestep can be slight or substantial, depending firstly on what the attacker is doing and secondly on what you intend to do to him. A large sidestep will avoid a wildly swinging attack but restrict your immediate counter to a kicking technique. A smaller sidestep will allow you to use faster hand techniques but it will expose you to more danger.

Fig 12

Twisting your hips as the weight comes down on your front foot turns you square on to the attacker and leaves all of your body weapon options available. Moving diagonally forwards to the attacker's blind side as he kicks leaves him very vulnerable. His body and yours are moving in opposite directions and a ridge hand strike across the front of his throat is particularly effective.

Evasion movements which utilise a turning motion of the body are additionally effective insofar as straight punches and kicks tend to glance off them without doing too much damage. If you have ever tried to poke a stick at a rotating treadmill in a children's playground you will know exactly what is meant.

It is as well to couple evasion with a block. You may wrongly evade into the path of an attack and if this happens, a blocking technique will protect you from otherwise certain injury. What are blocking techniques? They are extensions of the guard which you adopt (see Chapter 6) and work by interposing a limb into the path of the attack. If you heed the principles of redirection of force, you will not try to meet the attack head-on because whomsoever of you has the strongest bone structure will win (*fig 12*). Instead you must meet the attacking technique at an angle and redirect it. If the attack is vigorous, then don't be surprised if your re-direction completely unbalances the attacker.

After a great deal of consideration, we have chosen only two blocks for the Advanced Self Defence Course. These are the 'Slap block' and the 'Circular block'. The first uses the palm of the hand to deflect an attempted grab or punch. The block strikes to the side of the incoming technique and knocks it off course. For maximum deflection with minimum effort, the block must make contact close to the attacking wrist where leverage is greatest. Slapping block almost always uses the leading hand. This is closest to the opponent and has the shortest distance to travel. It is therefore very quick.

Slapping block can be used at quite long distances (*fig 13*) in which case it is delivered with a nearly straight elbow. Keep your shoulders relaxed and throw the hand at its target as though doing a straight punch. As it is about to connect, tighten the hand with a spasm, so it knocks the incoming technique to one side. Curl the fingers slightly so if necessary they can quickly close on a sleeve.

Slapping block is also an excellent short-range deflection and in this mode, it is used closer to the body with a 90° flexion of the elbow. For best effect, it is accompanied by a side step and hip twist motion that rolls the body with the incoming technique. For maximum coverage, hold your arm so the extended fingers are just on your hairline (*fig 14*). This version, coupled with a twisting action and a simultaneous lower circular block with the other arm covers virtually the whole of the body and head.

13   Fig 14

Fig 15   Fig 16   Fig 17

Circular block is a wide-ranging single or double arm block that stops just about any incoming technique. Used properly, it will allow you to even stand your ground in the face of a rush-in attack because it is so effective at redirecting force that the attacker can literally spin off you and lose balance.

Move your arms in contra-rotating circles and keep them virtually straight with fingers held firmly together and thumbs tucked in (*figs 15, 16, & 17*). The block is most effective when it catches an incoming technique between the rising arms and carries it up and out to one side. If a kick is deflected to the floor by a circular block, the attacker's stance is immediately stabilised and he can begin throwing punches. If it is lifted up instead, his balance is disturbed and a fast step forwards can tip him onto his back.

To be effective in this mode, the blocking arms must be held away from the body at all times (*fig 18*) and safety is preserved by moving body weight back over the rear leg. This is in contrast with slapping block which works best when combined with a sideways evasion.

Circular block is also effective when practised with one arm. In an upward sweep it will deflect a descending strike to the head (*fig 19*). In descending mode it can hook a punch down and to the side (*fig 20*). As it rises from a low side position, it can scoop up a straight kick. Single arm blocks are strengthened by hip rotation and body twisting evasions as are used for the slapping block.

Fig 19

Fig 20

8

The Body as a Weapons System

Most people thinking of fighting instinctively close their fists. It may surprise you to know that the fist is not the best weapon to use for a number of reasons. The first is that the delicate knuckles are protected only by a thin layer of skin and both are well provided with pain receptors. A hard impact with someone's head is almost certain to skin the knuckles and cause severe pain without knocking him out.

Secondly, few people can really roll their fingers tightly into the palm of the hand so they crunch up painfully on impact. Thirdly it is always a problem to locate the thumb safely. Tuck it into the palm and it sprains when the fist thuds home. Put it to the side of the index finger and it will invariably catch in someone's sleeve and get yanked back.

Fourthly the impact of a hard landing will produce a recoil effect which highlights incorrectly aligned joints such as the wrist. Unless the wrist is locked rigid and/or aligned with the bones of the forearm, the result will always be a painful wrist.

For all these faults, the fist can be used as a body weapon if it is both correctly formed and used against a vulnerable target.

Fig 21

Fig 22

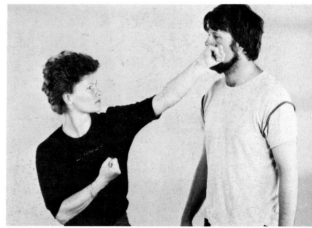

Begin by extending your fingers and thumb. Curl the fingers down and roll them into the palm. Close your thumb across the index and middle finger. Look at the correctly formed fist in profile (*fig 21*). See how the knuckles form a right angle with the back of the hand. Contrast this with a poorly formed fist where the middle knuckles of the fingers will make a painful first contact with the target and the wrist will bend on impact.

If you value your long fingernails, you will never be able to make a really tight fist though what you can manage may still be effectively used in other ways. If your fingernails are not that long, then there is no reason why you cannot get the required angle. Push the fingers back by pressing down onto flat surfaces with your fist.

Holding a correct fist is exhausting and once you can form it correctly, practise holding it loosely and then suddenly clenching it tightly for an instant. See how quickly you can snap your open hand into a fully formed fist. This is one of the components of an effective punch.

The normal application of the fist is with the knuckles. It is also possible to use the back of the knuckles in a swinging back-hand strike (*fig 22*). The little finger edge of the rolled fist is also effective when used in a hammer like action (*fig 23*).

A useful low-energy variant of the closed fist is called 'One-knuckle fist' (*fig 24*). This is made by forming a normal fist and poking out the index finger. Press your thumb down against the middle joint of the index finger as you make impact. Use this configuration to apply pressure to a vulnerable part of the opponent's body.

Fig 23

Fig 24

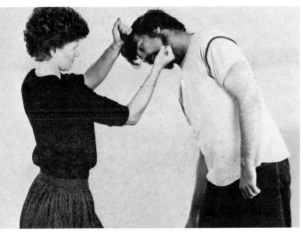

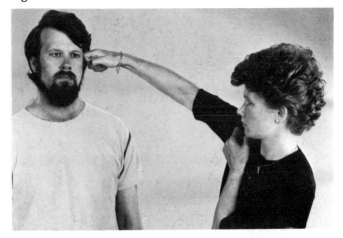

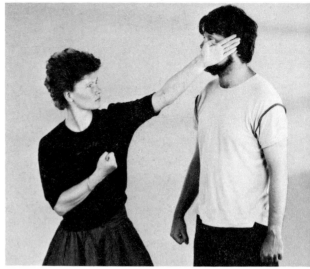

Fig 25

Fig 26

Use the open hand in a number of different ways to strike an attacker. Most familiar is the straightforward slap. To make this more than usually effective, keep the fingers together and the thumb lightly pressed to the side of the hand. Slightly cup the hand and just as you are about to make contact, suddenly tense it. Use a back handed slap too but land with the knuckles. Start by pointing your elbow at the target and hold your hand palm downwards-facing (*fig 25*). Fling your arm out and as it is about to make contact, strongly rotate the forearm whilst tensing the wrist (*fig 26*).

The little finger-side of the extended hand is sometimes called the 'Karate chop' but is more correctly named 'Knife-hand'. This is actually a difficult body weapon to use and is only effective against vulnerable targets. The trick is to land on the correct part of the hand (*fig 27*), avoiding the bones of the wrist and the base of the little finger. Deliver the strike with a strong rotation of the forearm, either going from a palm-up to palm-down configuration (*figs 28 & 29*), or the converse (*figs 30 & 31*).

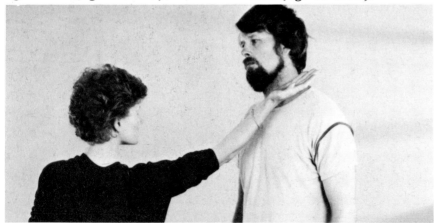

Fig 27

Fig 28

Fig 29

Fig 30

Fig 31

The thumb-side of the open hand is less often used though it is effective in a swinging and curling motion that brings it around the opponent's blind side. It is called 'Ridge-hand'.

Loosen your fingers and wrist and practise flicking your hand as though to shed drops of water. This is an extremely effective technique to use against the attacker's eyes. We are not suggesting for one minute that you try and plunge your fingertips into his eyes! This technique is intended only to make him blink.

Curl your fingers (*fig 32*) to form what is called 'Claw-hand'. Unlike the fist, this weapon is actually improved if you have long fingernails. Keeping your forearm and wrist relaxed, throw claw-hand at the attacker's face and as it contacts, dig your fingertips in hard.

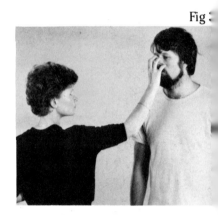

Fig :

Pull your wrist back to make 'Palm-heel' (*fig 33*). This is an excellent mid- and short range weapon for many reasons. First of all it is capable of being accelerated into a target. Secondly the impact surface is bony enough to inflict a sharp impact yet cushioned sufficiently to reduce self-inflicted injury. Thirdly, the troublesome wrist joint is eliminated. Palm-heel is typically used in a short jolting strike from close-quarters (*fig 34*).

Fig 33

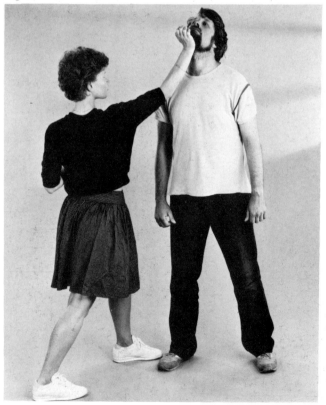

Fig 34

The elbow makes an excellent closer range body weapon and contrary to what you might imagine, it is difficult to catch your funny-bone. Use the tip of your elbow rather than your forearm because the latter is wasteful of impact energy, spreading it along a length of arm instead of over a small area. In case you are wondering what significance this has, ask yourself which would cause the more discomfort; pressure against your chest with the flat of your hand or the same pressure but channelled through just one knuckle.

The elbow can be used in three ways. The first is as a horizontal swinging blow to the side of the face/jaw (*fig 35*). The second is as a descending blow to the back of the neck/head (*fig 36*). The third is as an upswinging strike to the jaw of a taller opponent (*fig 37*) and the fourth as a horizontal straight thrust backwards into the ribs/solar plexus (*fig 38*). Remember to clench your fist tightly at the moment of impact.

The legs make good body weapons and because they have more mass than the arms, they are capable of delivering a heavier impact. They are slower to use than hand techniques and there are many situations where they are not the best weapons to use as the initial response. Use your legs when you are at a goodly distance from your opponent and don't kick if you are in punching range. Never kick above the waist unless you are a consummate and supple fighter and then remain on one leg for as short a time as possible.

Fig 35

Fig 36

Fig 37

Fig 38

The knee is a well known close-range weapon effective against the groin or thigh. Although the area immediately above the kneecap is well protected, be careful not to catch the kneecap itself against something hard! The force of impact is improved if the opponent is jerked forwards as the knee strike is made. If you manage to get two handfuls of hair or ear, pull the attacker's head down and bring your knee up sharply as you do so.

Fig 39

Fig 40

The instep of the foot is effective against the groin, being delivered with either a straight kick (*fig 39*) or a turning kick (*fig 40*). As a rule, straight kicks require accurate targeting whereas a turning kick can accommodate some error. Turn your toes downwards and try to bring your foot into one straight line with your shin. The impact area is between the front of the ankle and midway down the foot. Avoid making contact with the distal part of

Fig 41

Fig 42

Fig 43

your foot because if you are wearing light shoes, your toes can get painfully bent.

The outer edge of the heel is effective when used against the opponent's knee (*fig 41*) or instep (*fig 42*). It does however require accurate targeting. Use it from a sideways-on position by raising your knee to kicking height and driving the heel outwards and downwards into the side of your opponent's kneecap. Simultaneously lean away from a possible counter attack should the kick miss. The heel can also be used to stamp on the opponent's instep and against the opponent's groin (*fig 43*).

Flat of the foot is used in a thrusting manner to the knee (*fig 44*) or groin (*fig 45*). Bring your knee up smartly and jam the foot out, arching the back as you do, so as to project your hips forward without involving your face. Turn your foot outwards when aiming at the knee.

The head is an effective weapon when rammed into the opponent's nose or mouth but be sure to keep your face out of the way. Use the upper part of your forehead and tuck your chin in. Clench your teeth and pull your tongue back out of harm's way.

The teeth make fearsome close distance weapons and can be used either to break an attacker's grip, or to attack his face and ears. Do not waste your efforts against a well-muscled limb because people with a high pain tolerance can withstand even a hard bite. The thumb- and finger joints are particularly susceptible though you must use your other hand to guard your face.

Fig 44

Fig 45

Making Your Presence Felt

If you have ever pushed a car you will know that you have to lean into the push, brace with your feet firmly against the floor and heave and grunt. You are giving energy to the car and when enough is pumped in, its resistance to movement is overcome and it begins rolling. Once it is moving, the energy needed to keep it rolling is less than that needed to start it from standstill.

Though pushing a car is not a particularly good analogy, certain parts do hold true in a self defence situation. If you are going to hit someone hard enough to be effective, you must put enough effort into it. If you are a large person, that effort will not be difficult to come by but if you are small-boned, then it becomes necessary for you to achieve the same result but by a different route.

Regardless of the technique you are to use – be it strike or hold – you must be correctly balanced. Try and push a heavy car whilst standing on one leg or not leaning into it and you'll see what we mean. Your feet have to grip the floor and your body angle must be correct. Keep your knees slightly bent so they can straighten into the delivery, absorbing any tendency for the force being applied to rebound back through you.

When you push at the car, your stance and body position is set to maximise energy input and were the car to shoot off, you'd fall flat on your face. Similarly if you miss with a maximum energy strike you must expect to have to frantically scrabble to regain balance afterwards and that is why such strikes should not be used as the opening gambit of a self defence response. To be sure there are martial artists who can fire off impressive punches and fast, high kicks at nothing at all and yet remain perfectly poised. Be not disheartened! This is simply because the techniques are modified to allow this – but at the expense of effectiveness.

People using a lot of force often grunt with the exertion of it. This is because the muscles are tensed up, and the breath is held. As this explodes out of the lungs, driven by the action of the chest muscles and diaphragm, it produces a short, sharp grunt. As your maximum energy technique is about to land, allow yourself to breathe out in this sudden and violent way. It helps to develop maximum power.

Maximum energy strikes accelerate at the greatest rate your body is capable of generating. Even a light object can cause injury if it is thrown hard enough. Therefore whatever strike you use, get it moving as fast as possible. To do this, keep the muscles of the uninvolved parts relaxed. No sprinter could reach maximum speed if he or she kept their arms and chest muscles tightly contracted as they ran. Similarly, you will never be able to propel your arm or leg quickly enough if you are tense.

Try and throw your fist away from your body as though to shot-putt. Pull your arm back first to cock the technique and concentrate weight on your back leg (*fig 46*). Drive down with the ball of your rear foot and twist your hips around so they face the front – but leave your arm cocked (*fig 47*). This stretches the muscles in your back and sides, and loads them with energy. As this stretch builds to its maximum, release your shoulder and let it twist to the front, flinging your punching arm forwards and into the target. Your punching hand stays loose until the moment of impact when it suddenly and dramatically tightens into a fist (*fig 48*). This tightening action injects a final thrust of power.

As you twist into the punch, let your bodyweight lunge forwards even though in so doing your rear foot may lift clear of the ground. This allows the fist a couple of extra inches of travel without reducing its effectiveness and because the body is travelling behind the punch, the shock of impact is easily absorbed by its energy of movement.

Fig 46

Fig 47

Fig 48

Fig 49   Fig 50   Fig 51

It may be that you simply don't have the opportunity to perform all these gyrations. Perhaps you are sitting in a chair; then what? The answer is that you use those elements which are available to you and target the technique onto a vulnerable area. Whip your shoulder in behind the punch (*figs 49 & 50*), leaving your fist open until the last instant. Let your wrist relax so your hand droops during the initial phases and as the fist pulls tight, lock the wrist also. This increases the impact energy of the technique.

The trick is to keep uninvolved muscles totally relaxed during the delivery. The terminal spasm as your fist connects must be localised in the muscles of the forearm. Practise getting this localisation by gripping your fist tightly and then repeatedly and quickly flexing your elbow.

Though less powerful than the first punch delivery system, this latter method has two advantages. The first is that it can be used from any stance and the second is that it can be used over a very short distance. The longer a punch is in flight, the more opportunity there is to recognise and evade it. However, a punch travelling less than a foot is more difficult to react effectively to.

We have used the term 'punch' throughout for convenience but these same two systems will work for any straight line hand technique such as the palm-heel strike.

Fig 52

Fig 53

There is another class of hand technique which uses a rotational motion of the body. An effective parody of the movement appears frequently in the tv puppet show 'The Muppets' and is the speciality of Miss Piggy. In old Westerns, the fully fledged technique was called the 'haymaker'. The strike – be it slap, knife-hand, ridge-hand or punch, travels in an arc and is more difficult than the straight punch to stop if it misses.

The technique is 'wound up' by the hips twisting whilst the punching side remains pulled back (*fig 51*). This creates considerable tension in the spinal and chest muscle, loading them with potential energy in the process. When this energy is released, the punching shoulder slingshots around and the punch rises up and out into the target. The punching arm is bent at first but acceleration soon unwinds it. Extra power is injected by swinging the non-punching arm and pulling it back to the hip (*fig 52*).

The swinging punch is very powerful and because it follows a curved path, it is difficult to block (*fig 53*). On the other hand, it is easily recognised at an early stage because of the rather obvious body language which accompanies it. If it misses, it takes too long to recover.

Fig 54

Fig 55

Fig 56

The hook is a compromise technique which curves over a shorter distance than the swing. Bring both arms to a high guard position (*fig 54*) and keep your hands open and relaxed. Twist your right hip around, so the right heel rises from the floor. Keep your shoulders square as you do this (*fig 55*). Withdraw your left hand and allow your right shoulder to swing around behind the hip. As your hand is about to connect, lock it into palm-heel, a normal punch (*fig 56*) or suddenly bend it at the elbow to produce an elbow strike. A strike like this to the side of the opponent's jaw can easily produce a knockout.

Upwards travelling thrusts such as the short distance palm-heel and upwards travelling elbow strike use the same principles except they are accompanied by a straightening of the slightly bent knees. Downward travelling strikes like hammer-fist or descending elbow strike are made more powerful if the knees are slightly bent at the moment of impact.

Kicks are invariably stronger than hand techniques but they are slower and easier to avoid. There are less little tricks to be employed in enhancing impact but do keep non-involved musculature relaxed throughout and watch for your shoulders hunching up as you kick – this is a sure sign that your shoulders are too tense. If the kick misses, pull it back quickly so a stable stance can be re-established. For this we rely upon a spring-like action of the knee joint.

Consider first the front thrust kick. This is powered by a piston-like thrusting out of the heel assisted by the hips which move

57   Fig 58   Fig 59

forward behind it. If the hips don't drive forwards hard enough, the kick is weakened. If the back arches too much, recoil can knock you backwards off balance.

Bring your kicking knee to the correct height. If you want to kick the opponent in the groin, then raise your knee above the level of his groin so your kick is delivered slightly downwards into the target. Thrust kick is slower than snap kick but it cannot be trapped the way the latter can by the opponent closing his thighs on the rising foot.

If the kick is obviously going to fall short, don't try and make it over-reach because by doing so it will be weakened and your balance imperilled. Instead make a slight dragging hop forwards on the bent supporting leg as the knee is rising to kicking height. Not only does this close range, it can also add a bonus of power if you correctly synchronise the moment of impact with the settling of the supporting heel. Make sure you don't jump into the air before you kick; a short slide is all that is needed.

Snapping kicks use a different method of developing energy. Like the high-speed strike, the ball of the kicking foot drives down against the floor, so the heel rises. As this is happening, the hips turn square on to the opponent (*fig 57*). The back is arched and gives up its energy as the kicking knee rises to the correct height (*fig 58*). As the knee reaches operational height, the lower leg lashes out and at the moment of impact, the foot is held rigid with the toes downturned (*fig 59*). Allow the natural spring of the knee joint to bring the foot back after impact.

Fig 60   Fig 61   Fig 62

Turning kick uses the same mechanism but with rotation of the supporting leg. At first the action is exactly the same as an orthodox snap kick and this is as it should be since the object is to disguise your technique from the opponent until it's too late. As the knee is rising fast, the supporting leg begins to rotate (*fig 60*) and the rising foot is brought into an arc. The kicking hip rises with the knee and tends to roll over the top of the supporting leg. Note how much the supporting leg has rotated and the way the body is leaning away from the impact. This is useful in that it keeps your face away from counter-attacks. As the knee reaches the correct height, the lower leg is lashed out with the toes down-turned (*fig 61*).

Use turning kick when a direct kick is blocked because of your line (for explanation of 'line' refer to Chapter 6).

Side thrust kick harnesses both the weight of the descending limb and a thrusting action provided by swivelling hips to generate its power. Raise the knee to the height of your own groin (higher if you are shorter than your opponent). Drive the heel diagonally down and away from your body, swivelling on the supporting leg as you do so (*fig 62*). Note the way the body has leaned to counterbalance the weight of the kicking leg. Note also that the supporting foot has swivelled further than it does in a turning snap kick. It is the combination of these two factors that stops you from falling into the opponent. After your heel makes contact, pull your leg back against your body before setting it down.

If you are slightly too far away, drag sideways as your knee rises to kicking height. Combine the thrust of your descending heel with rotation of the supporting leg to realise maximum force.

It doesn't matter which impact technique you use, hit the target whilst the limb is still accelerating. As it travels to its point of maximum reach, acceleration drops sharply and energy is shed. Practise your striking techniques against an impact pad held by your partner. This will give a very close approximation to the sensation of hitting a human mass. Because the pad is made from resilient foam, your feet and hands are not damaged.

Your partner should lean slightly into the blow, holding the pad at chest height. For kicks, wind your arms through the straps and hold the pad against your upper arm. Don't angle the pad so the incoming technique skids off it. When you feel confident about hitting the pad hard, have your partner advance and pull back to give you experience with ranging strikes against a moving target. You will find that you have to launch a technique early if the opponent is advancing, so the target has moved into range as your technique is reaching maximum speed.

If you close into grappling range with your attacker, beware of wasting your energy in a direct confrontation. If you try to resist his pull, the stronger of you will win. If you begin to resist him and then as he pulls a little harder, suddenly step into him, you can cause him to lose balance. If he tries to push you, begin by resisting but then pull him sharply towards you.

You must apply a lock or hold as quickly as possible if it is to be successful. Tense your muscles strongly as power is applied and do not give the opponent time to realise what you are doing, by keeping him moving all the time. For example, his push forwards is turned into a pull and before he can recover balance, the throw or hold has been executed. This requires far less energy than starting a throw from cold and is analogous to redirecting the car once it is moving. As a matter of fact it is a skilful person indeed who can stand their ground and pit technique against brute strength. Where movement is restricted, rely instead upon an initial distracting technique.

Throws rely not upon power as such but on timing, balance and leverage. Whereas the ideal build for an effective puncher/kicker is tall and slim, the best shape for the thrower is short and squat, with a low centre of gravity.

10

Where to Attack

A strong punch is unlikely to have its maximum effect if it lands on the shoulder-blades. Similarly an immobilising joint lock applied to the shoulder is not likely to work unless the person applying it is very strong. Whatever technique you use, it must be applied to an appropriate part of the opponent's body.

High impact striking techniques are usually aimed at such targets as the nose, jaw, throat, solar plexus, kidneys, groin, kneecaps and insteps. The nose is richly supplied with blood vessels and sensory nerve endings. A sharp blow against it with palm-heel or hammer-fist can provoke floods of tears with resulting obscured vision. The jaw is often regarded as the brain's 'fuse' and a sharp blow on it can daze or produce unconsciousness. Blows which land slightly to the side of the jaw sharply rotate the head and are more likely to cause a knockout.

Fig 6

The mouth is not a good target because of the teeth. Though these can be painfully damaged, they can also cause serious injury to the body weapon used. No matter how often they are brushed, the teeth harbour germs which can produce particularly nasty infected lacerations.

The throat is a vulnerable part of the body, carrying as it does the windpipe and major bloodvessels supplying the brain. The windpipe is a cartilaginous tube which can be compressed by the thumbs or forearm, so the passage of air is impeded. Such strangulation holds cause the victim to struggle violently and are more difficult to keep applied than the vee-strangulation method applied by the crook of the elbow (*fig 63*). This applies pressure to the sides of the neck and though the windpipe is not closed, the flow of arterial blood to the brain is reduced and unconsciousness quickly ensues without the onset of such violent struggles as are encountered in the orthodox strangle.

The solar plexus is a concentration of nerves located in the centre of the lower chest. A sharp and penetrating blow there by such as an elbow strike causes difficulty in breathing. The kidneys lie above the waist and on either side of the spine. They are not targets of choice for the average person because the level of impact needed to have an effect is quite high and best administered by a strong kick.

The groin is very vulnerable because only a small impact is needed to produce a big effect. Not many men can ignore impact to the testicles and the effect of a strike there spreads rapidly to the muscles of the stomach and chest. A single hard blow to the groin is enough to bring the most savage attacker to a complete stop. Even a feint to the groin provides a useful distraction.

The kneecap is vulnerable to a hard impact and it helps if you are wearing steel-tipped heels. If you can see it clearly, the instep is an easy target for a short range stamping kick. We make that point because instep attack is sometimes suggested as a method of escaping from a rear strangle. We don't advise this because if you can't see where the attacker's feet are, then you are just doing a spot of futile tap dancing as consciousness fades.

Low energy strikes can be used against areas with a high density of sensory nervous tissue and are ideal for those situations where a fully-fledged self defence technique is inappropriate. They need little setting up and are not stance/distance critical to the same extent as high energy strikes. This·is very useful if you are sitting down or are otherwise unable to accelerate the strike to a high speed. Unfortunately, they must be accurately targeted and effectiveness is often reduced if the attacker is wearing clothing which covers the target area.

The eyes are very vulnerable and well protected by an automatic response that closes them tightly and pulls the head back out of trouble whenever a fast-moving technique approaches. This aversion reaction is very useful in creating a short distraction during which you can use a more effective technique. You must however actually aim to strike the eyes, or your hand will not approach closely enough to trigger this aversion mechanism. If you use the flicking motion described in the section entitled 'Body Weapons' then even if you happen to catch the cornea, you are unlikely to cause permanent injury.

Even the closed eyes can be used to force an attacker to relinquish a bear-hug. Place your thumbs against his eyeballs and press inwards, using smoothly increasing pressure. This will force him to break his grip.

The filtrum of the nose is that plate of cartilage which separates

Fig 65

Fig 64

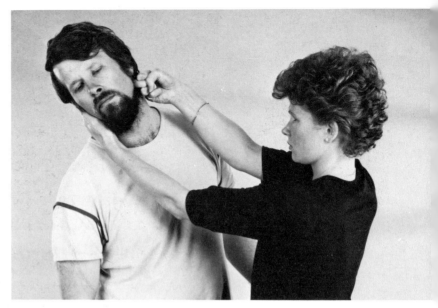

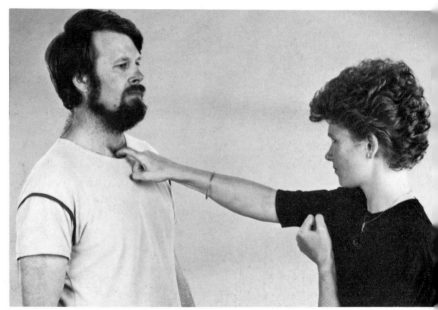

Fig 6

your nostrils. If you rest the heel of your hand on the attacker's upper lip – just over the front incisors – and push upwards and slightly inwards, you will drive the attacker's head back and break out of a bear-hug (*fig 64*). You can also reach over from behind and pull an attacker off his victim by hooking your fingers under the filtrum and tugging his head back.

Just below the angle of the jaw is another pressure point which causes severe pain when compressed by one-knuckle fist (*fig 65*). Apply increasing pressure and corkscrew the knuckle to get the best effect. The collar-bones meet in the midline of the chest and immediately above them at the base of the neck is another pressure point. Press in with your index finger and hook back slightly to inflict pain (*fig 66*).

Fig 68

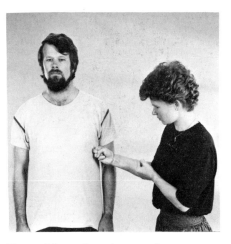

g 67

Broad bands of muscle pass out from the base of the neck over the top of the shoulders. If you have a strong grip, stand behind the opponent and place your thumbs close to the base of his neck and curl your fingers into the front part of the same muscles, just above the collar bones. If you now squeeze tightly, you will cause severe pain and drive the opponent to his knees (*fig 67*).

Use the one-knuckle punch also against the sides of the ribs (*fig 68*) and corkscrew inwards to produce acute pain.

The groin can be attacked with a low energy strike such as a slap and like the eyes, a powerful feint there produces an aversion reaction. Typically the head is brought down and the face becomes vulnerable to an elbow strike (*figs 69 & 70*). It is generally not possible to grasp the testicles because trousers get in the way but simple pressure alone will interfere with the attacker's concentration.

g 69

Fig 70

Most people have a pad of flesh which can be squeezed up at the top and to the inside of the thigh. If this is pinched hard, acute pain is caused. Additional encouragement can be given by twisting the trapped flesh whilst squeezing it tightly.

Holds work on the principle of leverage. A small force applied to the end of a long lever can produce a big response. However in a self defence application, the object being levered against is using muscle power to resist and an incorrectly applied hold may be shrugged off because the attacker is stronger. The aim must therefore be to use leverage effectively to attack the weaker joints such as those of the fingers or wrist. Stronger persons can also attack the elbow.

The joint can be bent in the direction it normally moves – but further than is customary such as with the 'Gooseneck' (*fig 71*), or it can be forced against its normal direction of movement as with the 'Arm lever' (*fig 72*). Both of these can be made more painful without increasing the effort needed simply by using a longer lever. In the case of the gooseneck, slide your grasp further down towards the knuckles. In the case of the arm lever, move the fulcrum over the elbow joint.

Fig 71

Fig

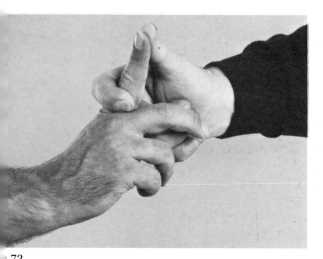

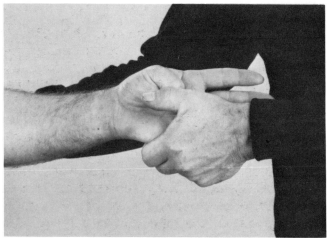

73

Fig 74

These principles are clearly seen too in finger holds. The first type anchors the lower part of the finger whilst forcing the top back (*fig 73*). The second forces the thumb to over-bend by driving it back and upwards (*fig 74*).

A hold need not cause pain on the point of application. In a twisting gooseneck type of hold (*fig 75*), the bent wrist is used as a lever against the two bones of the forearm, causing them to jam up together.

Fig 75

11

Safe Training

Before you get going and start bashing everyone in sight, it's a good idea to consider a few matters of safety. First of all are you fit enough to be able to train? When was the last time you took any form of physical exercise? If you are over forty years of age and have previously led a sedentary lifestyle, it might be a good idea to see your doctor first and get a clean bill of health. Unaccustomed training can show up a physical weakness with unfortunate results.

You may still train if you suffer from hay fever, asthma or diabetes but do keep your medication in easy reach. In fact you can train regardless of disability, with the exception of haemophilia. Regrettably the stresses and odd knocks in training can lead to haemorrhages and so the haemophiliac must avoid all self defence and martial arts training with the exception of Tai chi chuan.

If you suffer from a chronic illness and are not sure whether you should train, consult your doctor first.

Having discovered that you are fit and capable of taking up a self defence course, next ensure that you join a good club. The best way to ensure that you do this is to apply to the Martial Arts Commission as explained in Chapter 3. By joining the right club, you will automatically become insured against loss of earnings through being damaged, or against being sued when you damage your partner. Whilst either eventuality is thankfully rare, it cannot be absolutely ruled out and the relevant insurance is no bad thing to have.

If you use the techniques in this book to train at home, do make sure you have a large enough space to practise in and a soft enough floor to land on. Concrete floors are dangerous to practise on because of the risk of falling onto your head. A good thick carpet is the very least you may train safely on. Clear the practice area of obstacles such as chairs or tables over which you can trip. Keep away from glass doors and sharp edges.

Your training partner needs to be well briefed on what you are going to do next. We have so often seen the situation where the attacker is expected to do a certain move that allows the defender to practice an arranged response but doesn't! This is all the more important if your partner is much larger (or much smaller) than you are. Large people generate a lot of power without ever knowing it and can cause injury with what is to them a well controlled technique.

Practise the technique slowly at first, until you are able to link all the moves together properly. Only then should the tempo of training increase. Get your partner to work at a mutually satisfactory speed – one which you can handle and not become dispirited. Make sure the attack is on target and as realistic as possible bearing in mind your current level of ability. Never allow your partner to aim off-target or to use a weak technique because this will build a faulty response.

What you are trying to achieve is an increase in your skill level, so you can eventually put a complex technique into unerring action. At first this will be very difficult because you will be unused to the technique and each of its interlinking parts will have to be considered separately. It is only through constant repetition that the facility to perform the whole technique in one fast flowing sequence can be built up.

12
Fit to Train

The typical self defence situation is likely to be resolved one way or the other in a matter of seconds of explosive action rather than minutes – unless of course you are running away from your pursuer and want to stay in front of him! It is extremely unlikely that your encounter will turn into a toe-to-toe punch up that goes on for two or three rounds without respite. This sort of thing happens only in the cinema.

You will need to act quickly and powerfully for your response to succeed and this in itself requires a certain level of physical fitness. Having said that, training for self defence does require a measure of fitness if you are going to be able to repeat and repeat yet again a technique until you have got it right. You will be required to do a technique not just once – and that's it, but a number of times against a partner.

Of course, you can always cheat. If you don't put much effort into the technique you can save a bit of energy. If you persuade your partner to take it easy you need not work so hard. Unfortunately, applying techniques incorrectly is easier to do than getting them right. Dealing with an opponent – albeit a training partner – who is taking it easy will equip you only with the means of dealing with a helpful attacker. Both of these malpractices will rob your training of its value and instil incorrect and weak responses.

You must train hard to get the benefit from instruction you are receiving. If you find yourself puffing and panting by the time the session is only half over, then you will be so busy coping with the discomfort that the essence of what you are trying to perfect will pass you by. It therefore follows that a certain level of fitness is essential to self defence training.

You must be fit enough to last through the training – i.e., have enough endurance, and those parts of your body which you are repeatedly using must be able to cope. You must be able to move quickly when making a response, selecting the correct evasion or sidestep and executing it smartly without falling over your feet. This requires agility. Your self defence techniques must be performed with the necessary speed and strength – the combination of which is called power and your joints be capable of bending to the right amount and in the right direction. This last requirement is called suppleness.

You may already be a remarkably fit soul, in which case well done and keep up the training. If you aren't, then it is as well to begin a series of exercises to improve your level of fitness. A word to the wise, however; don't overdo training at first. Get yourself used to a gradually increasing physical work load over a period of time and you will reduce the aches and pains that will surely otherwise ensue.

Don't limit these exercise sessions by attaching them to your once- or twice a week self defence lessons. Make a habit of doing about twenty minutes of exercise at least every other day. The form this should take is a continuous low-intensity activity which you can maintain for the whole period. This type of exercising will tone up your heart and improve the supply of oxygen to working muscles.

Jogging is acceptable for this type of training, though you may find the constant thumping of feet against tarmac produces pains in your ankles and knees. If you like jogging, try running over grass – it's much less likely to cause leg aches and pains. If you are already a fairly active jogger, then try the wrist and ankle weights which are now available. These are light weights (or so they feel at the beginning of your jog!), encased in washable terry-towelling type material which is easy to keep clean.

The object of this type of training is to get your heart beating at a rate where if sustained, it will give a good training effect. If you run too fast/far, then your heart rate will increase above the training band and soon you will become exhausted and be forced to stop. Remember, the target of your supplementary fitness training is to complete a twenty minute exercise session. If you are very unfit, you will not be capable of running either very quickly or very far but that really doesn't matter – as long as you complete the period.

Some people find jogging difficult because they have the wrong shape – there is too much to flap about and cause discomfort. Such people should try swimming or cycling as an alternative. For those with a little money, a good rowing or cycling machine removes the last possible excuse for not training. In the final analysis, it's all down to motivation and if you don't have it, no exercise regime can be maintained.

Fig 76

Fig 77

Fig 78

It sometimes helps if you keep a little training diary, noting the distance you went for the time you trained. The continual slight improvement this soon reveals may well provide the motivation you need.

Assuming that you take this regular exercise programme on board, you will find the following additional schedule very helpful indeed for extracting the maximum benefit from your self defence training. Used before your self defence lesson it will ensure that you are fully prepared for the rigours of training. It will gradually ease you from your normal level of activity to that encountered in training, so discomfort is lessened and training benefit increased. It will gently work muscles in preparation for the demands that will be placed upon them, whilst simultaneously taking joints through their full range of movement.

Fig 81

Begin by running on the spot, raising your knees high and letting your arms move naturally. Hop twice on the spot with one leg, then the other (*figs 76 & 77*). Stand with your feet a shoulder width apart and your feet turned slightly outwards (*fig 78*). Drop down into a half-squat (*fig 79*) and pause there before driving yourself up again. Do not go below a half squat because this places an inordinate strain on the knee joint. Aim to bend your knee through no more than 90° in all.

Pause during the half-squat because it makes the exercise slightly more difficult to do. If you drop down and immediately bounce back up, you make use of additional muscle power which helps defeat the object of this exercise.

Fig 79

Fig 80

Jump up and down, keeping your arms to your sides and springing up off the balls of your feet (*fig 80*). If you feel particularly energetic, on every tenth jump leap as high as you can and pull your knees up against your chest.

Burpees are excellent exercises for warming the whole body up. Start from an upright position (*fig 81*) and drop straight down onto your haunches, with tips of fingers touching the ground (*fig 82*). Shoot your legs out behind you in one movement, taking the weight of your upper body on straight arms (*fig 83*). Without a pause, jump back in with your feet so they are once more under your body (*fig 84*) and jump upright. Repeat the cycle of moves for up to twenty-five repetitions.

82

Fig 83

Fig 84

Fig 85

Fig 86

Fig 87

Star jumps are the last of this type of warm-up exercise. From an upright stance with feet a shoulder width apart, jump into the air and extend your arms and legs as far apart as you can (*fig 85*). Retrieve them before you touch down.

Do a series of short sprints, perhaps six metres long and at the end of each, come to a dead stop. Then take off in another direction. Follow this by jumping from side to side with alternating single leg leaps (*fig 86*) over a distance of perhaps 25 metres. Finally skip quickly forwards by swinging the advancing leg across the front of the other (*fig 87*).

Fig 88

Fig 89

By now you should be huffing and puffing a bit and wondering where on earth you're going to find enough energy to do the training itself. Don't worry – all you have been doing is to prepare your muscles for the demands of training. Proceed now with exercises designed to make your self defence techniques more powerful.

The first of these is the ubiquitous **press-up**. This is particularly good for strengthening upper body and arm muscles. Don't worry if you can't do even one because you can vary the exercise and still make it useful by dropping down onto your knees (*fig 88*). Otherwise support your body on the tips of your toes and the flats of your hands. Do keep your body in one straight line (*fig 89*) and don't sag in the middle or poke your bottom up in the air.

Lower yourself down until your chest brushes the floor (*fig 90*). Pause at this lowest position to get the best training effect and then firmly push yourself back up so your elbows straighten. Do not bounce down because this reduces the muscle effort needed to drive you back up. Do the exercise properly and as your muscles become tired, don't let it degenerate into merely bobbing up and down. Remember, it is better to do a small number of exercises correctly than a large number incorrectly!

Even if your upper body musculature is feeble, regular press-ups practice will strengthen it and soon you will be able to do at least 20 good ones. At this stage, you are ready to move on to developing your upper body power.

Drop down to the lowest press-ups position and after the customary pause, drive yourself up as hard and as quickly as you can. Aim to drive your hands clear of the floor and as you become more adept at this, clap them together (*fig 91*) before dropping back down. Don't expect to be able to do this exercise straight away.

Fig 90

Fig 91

Fig 92

Fig 93

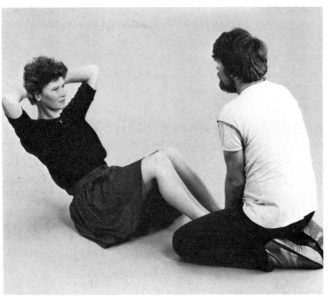

Fig 94

Fig 95

Concentrate next on strengthening your abdominal muscles using the exercise known as **sit-up**. To avoid damaging your lower back, bend your knees (*fig 92*). Clasp your hands behind your head but don't tug hard as you lever yourself up. All the required effort must come from the abdominal muscles.

Contrary to what you might think, it is only necessary to raise your upper body clear of the ground (*fig 93*). You don't have to rise so far that your chest touches your knees because this calls into play other muscles that do not need working in this particular way.

You might find that your upper body is heavy and as you try to lift off, your feet rise instead. This is quite common and can be overcome by hooking your feet underneath something, or by having a partner press down on your insteps (*fig 94*). Try not to jerk into the exercise and when you reach the position of highest lift, pause for a second before lowering yourself back. Don't flop down and do not spring back up immediately upon landing.

Aim to do at least twenty good sit-ups and when can, vary them by rotating your body so you touch your right knee with your left elbow (*fig 95*) and on the next rise, your left knee with your right elbow.

Roll onto your tummy and grasp hands in the small of your back. Alternatively lace them behind your head but be careful not to tug on your neck. Try to raise your chest clear of the ground, by arching your back (*fig 96*) and if your feet are the only parts that come off the ground, then get your partner to press down on your heels. Don't raise your shoulders too far because the straining involved can make you feel dizzy. This particular exercise is known as a hyper-extension.

Fig 96

Moving on yet again to a further series of exercises, we encounter one much praised by Doctor James Canney, the Chief Medical Officer of the Martial Arts Commission. Doctor Canney is fond of remarking how a waking cat efficiently prepares itself for potential imminent fight or flight by stretching its spine in a certain way, which is why we have called this exercise **'The Cat'**.

Take up a press-ups position but arch your back by pushing your bottom into the air as far as you can (*fig 97*). Bend your elbows, so your body skims forward just above the ground (*fig 98*). Then straighten your arms and drop your hips as low as they will go so your back now arches the reverse way (*fig 99*). From this position, assume the starting posture by reversing the sequence of movements.

Fig

Fig 97

Fig 98

Fig 99

101

Rather less exhausting but nevertheless useful for improving flexibility is the exercise we call **Side stretches**. Stand with your feet well apart and lower your body first to one side (*fig 100*), then to the other. The exercise is assisted if you use your arms to add weight to your upper body. Having said that, don't jerk into the stretch but rather ease yourself smoothly into the lowest position, hold it for a few seconds and then return to an upright position.

Curiously enough, a jerking motion will not assist muscles to stretch but will rather cause a reflexive tightening as the muscle attempts to protect itself from sudden and violent over-stretching.

Keep in the same stance and this time twist your body to one side (*fig 101*), then to the other. As we mentioned in the exercise above, move smoothly into the stretch, holding the position of maximum stretch for a couple of seconds. When you have done this exercise a dozen or so times to each side, lower your body forwards and let the weight of your arms gradually drag your upper body downwards (*fig 102*).

Don't worry if at first you can't touch the ground with your hands because some people have rather long legs and short arms. Persevere and you will succeed. When you can do it, lean through between your open legs and push your arms away from you (*fig 103*). Hold the lowest position for a couple of seconds before coming up. Go directly into a hyper-extension by forcing your hips forward and leaning back as far as you can (*fig 104*). Hold this too for a few seconds before repeating the exercise.

Fig 102

Fig 103

Fig 104

Place your hands on your hips and rotate your lower trunk in wide circles, moving first one way (*fig 105*), then the other. Move smoothly and make the circles as large as possible. Dip forwards with arms trailing down (*fig 106*) and swing your shoulders around in a wide circle that takes you first to the one side (*fig 107*), then into a hyper-extension and finally down the other side. When you reach the lowest point of the circle once more, pause briefly and then repeat the circle but this time in the opposite direction.

Fig 105

Fig 106

Begin working on your legs with a stretch performed from a wide stance (*fig 108*). Lower your weight over one knee and keep the other straight. As you bend your supporting knee, you will feel a slight pulling up the inside of your thigh. This is to be expected but be very careful not to overdo things by bouncing or by exceeding the point at which discomfort sets in. When you have reached the lowest point, hold it for a few seconds before straightening your supporting knee and reversing the stretch.

107

Fig 108

The next exercise goes a step further in that you sink onto one haunch. Lean forward and carry your hands out as counterweights. It is permissible to rest the heel of your extended leg on the ground but do try to keep your supporting foot flat. Lack of ankle flexibility may encourage you to lift your heel off the ground but this must be avoided.

When you have reached the position of greatest stretch, hold it for at least five seconds without bouncing. Then transfer your weight from one side to the other and repeat the exercise.

Fig 109

Fig 110

Sit down with your legs close together and out straight in front of you. Keep the backs of your legs pressed firmly to the ground as you lean forwards as far as possible. If it helps, grasp your heels and pull yourself down (*fig 109*) but if you have long legs and short arms – this might prove difficult! Hold yourself at the lowest point for at least five seconds before returning to an upright position.

There will be a tendency for the backs of your legs to rise from the ground as you lean forwards and this must be avoided at all costs or the exercise will lose its training effect. People who are quite stiff may find themselves merely nodding their heads up and down. This is also cheating and must be avoided.

When you can lean forward by a respectable amount, open your legs as far as you can and lean between them (*fig 110*). Remember to keep your knees straight and your head still. Hold the lowest position before rising once more to an upright position. Vary the exercise by inclining your body first to one knee (*fig 111*), then to the other.

Gather your feet close to your thighs. Lean between your knees and pull yourself smoothly down by grasping your feet (*fig 112*). Hold the lowest position and then return once more to an upright position. Repeat this exercise at least five times and avoid head-nodding.

Fig 112

111

Roll backwards onto your shoulders and extend your legs straight. Keep yourself steady by splaying your arms to either side (*fig 113*). Return to a sitting position and repeat the exercise. Vary it by opening your legs but keep your knees absolutely straight (*fig 114*).

When you can touch the ground with the tips of your toes, vary the training effect again, this time by bending your knees and dropping your legs first to one side (*fig 115*), then to the other.

Fig 113

Fig 114

Fig 115

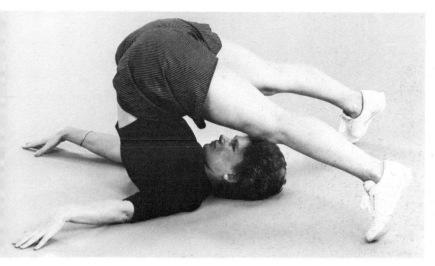

Fig 116   Fig 117

Kneel down with your feet extended and your back straight (*fig 116*). This is good for stretching the long muscles on the front of your thighs. It is also useful for ankle flexibility. It is best performed on a resilient floor so all the discomfort comes from the bits being stretched and not from uncushioned bones pressing into a hard floor.

When you can tolerate this quite well for several minutes, gradually lower yourself back until your shoulders are resting against the ground (*fig 117*) but don't let your knees rise off the ground. Use this and the preceding exercise to get your breath back after the more energy-demanding earlier exercises.

Some of the techniques you will learn involve twisting the wrists so it is a good idea to work on those particular joints. Begin by twisting your wrist so the little finger is brought towards the chest (*fig 118*). Apply firm but gentle pressure and then release before applying the same treatment to your other wrist. Point your fingers away from the body and try to rotate your hand palm-upwards (*fig 119*). Repeat this too on the other wrist. Turn your fingers downwards and pull back on your palm (*fig 120*). Repeat the exercise on the other wrist.

Fig 118   Fig 119   Fig 120

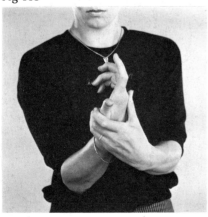
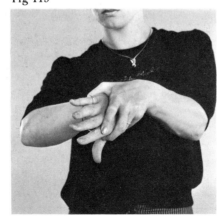
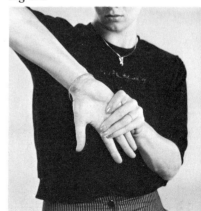

The ankle must not be omitted from the training schedule, so gather your one leg across the top of the other and take hold of your foot (*fig 121*). Rotate the ankle in a wide circle going first one way, then the other. Change legs and repeat the exercise.

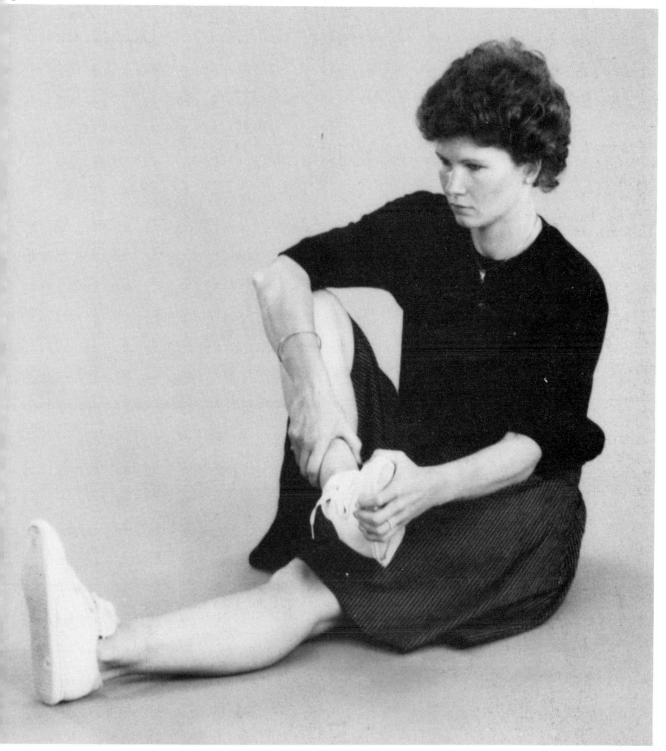

Fig 122

Fig 123

Fig 124

Stand upright and place your hands on your slightly bent knees. Move your legs in a wide circle, first one way (*fig 122*) – then the other. Stand upright and move your arms in slow and full contra-rotating circles (*figs 123, & 124*).

Fig 125

Fig 126

Fig 127

Complete your pre-training schedule with neck exercises. Drop your head first to one side (*fig 125*), then the other . Repeat this at least five times to each side. Twist your head one way (*fig 126*), then the other. Doing these too violently can quickly produce a headache, so use restraint.

Let your head fall onto your chest (*fig 127*) and then lift it up and back (*fig 128*). There is another neck exercise which consists of rolling the head around the shoulders in opposing circles but this can produce dizziness and is not recommended.

This then completes the pre-training schedule and you are now fully ready to take part in the self defence class. As you will have noticed, there are quite a few exercises so allow yourself at least twenty minutes before the start of the session. It may be that the self defence coach will want you to go through a sequence of exercises too but it is unlikely he/she will have enough valuable time to spend on a thorough warm-up such as has been suggested.

Don't let yourself get cold during practice and when there are lulls in training, slip on a tracksuit top or begin jogging on the spot. At the end of training, spend at least ten minutes on a cool-down sequence of exercises. This is very important because if you observe it, you will be less likely to suffer aches and pains in the days after training.

ig 128

The object of the cool-down is to gradually return your muscles from their elevated activity state, to one approaching normal. The fluids and waste products which have built up during training can be pumped out by selecting some of the whole-body exercises described at the beginning of this programme, though they must be performed at a slower and gradually reducing pace. Complete the cool-down with gentle stretching exercises to work the back and thighs.

Soon after the session, replenish fluid lost during training but avoid anything containing alcohol because if you are dehydrated, even a single glass of lager can have a marked effect and you may not be safe then to drive.

13
Falling Safely

During any self defence situation there is a distinct possibility that you will fall, trip, or be thrown to the floor. Therefore practise falling with the intention of developing a method to minimise injury. Begin your practice on a soft or springy floor because although you won't be attacked on one, repeated falls during practice will be cushioned.

The object when falling safely is to try and slow the release of kinetic energy in your falling body by converting the downwards motion into a more complex form. However, you may be actually hurled to the floor and in this case, the only recourse that remains is for you to try and land on a part of your body that is well cushioned with muscle or fat.

Begin by practising to fall backwards. Squat down on a cushioned surface and roll backwards. Tuck your chin into your chest and allow your hands to splay to either side (*fig 129*).

Fig 129

Because your spine is curved forwards, the energy of falling is gradually used up as you roll onto your back. When you are confident at doing this technique, start from a half squat and by degrees come to an upright starting position. Always bend your knees as you overbalance backwards because this helps the roll back to occur.

Next practise falling to the side and begin by lying on your back. Roll onto your left side and then twist back, slapping the floor hard with the palm of your right hand. Fling your right arm well out of the body and take care to keep the point of the elbow away from first contact with the ground (*fig 130*). Roll back the other way and slap down with your left arm. When you feel reasonably confident, go into a full squat position and overbalance yourself to the right. Curve your body away from the fall and slap the ground with your right hand.

Fig 130

Fig 131

Fig 132

Fig 1:

Stand upright and swing your right foot across the front of the left, throwing yourself to the right (*fig 131*). Drop your hip down first and curl your head up and away from the fall. Slap the ground as you land and keep perfectly relaxed throughout (*fig 132*). When falling from a height, don't land on your outstretched arm because this can cause a fracture of the forearm bones.

Falling forwards uses a roll-out motion to soak up kinetic energy. Reach down with your right arm and tuck your head well in (*fig 133*). Roll forwards onto your forearm and shoulder so you turn a somersault (*fig 134*). Gather your feet in to break the forward roll at that point. It is possible to roll-out in safety from quite a high speed, as long as you remember to keep your head tucked down. As you get to feel more confident, increase the speed at which you enter the roll-out.

Fig 134

14

Working From a Distance

We will now consider the application of those concepts we studied in earlier sections by using them in a one-to-one pre-arranged practice. To benefit from this, you need the assistance of a trusted partner who can be relied on both to cooperate with you and at the same time, make you work hard. The attacker of choice is a large person, perhaps a male because the object is to give you a sense of what it might be like when facing a large and aggressive person.

Your attacker must work at a speed you can manage and when you succeed in stopping most of his attacks, he should gradually speed up and make them more powerful. He must attack to a target and not yield to an ineffective response because if he does, then you will learn only how to deal with an ineffectual opponent. If like you, your partner wishes to learn the self defence system, then we suggest you take it in turns to be attacker/defender. Play each role for three or four techniques and then turn-about.

In this section you will be practising how to deal with the attacker whom you have kept at a safe distance by operating the instructions given in the section 'Keep on the Right Foot'. He cannot reach you without first stepping forwards and you will use this valuable cue to respond correctly.

You must react as he begins to move; any delay and his attack will catch you unprepared. Some say that the attacker's eyes give a clue to imminent and forceful movement – they momentarily narrow just as the body acts. Others advise you to watch the attacker's mouth, since this thins, or purses at the same instant. On the other hand, you will never be hit by the attacker's eyes or mouth so it may be as well if you try to keep as much of him under scrutiny as your peripheral vision will allow.

Have your partner take up left stance and stand in the same posture, facing him from a correct distance and line. With as little warning as possible he steps forward, advancing with his right

Fig 135   Fig 136

leg and reaching for your lapel with his right hand. Step smartly to the side and out of line, slapping his arm to one side as you do so (*fig 135*). Don't concentrate overly much on blocking since your step, if done correctly, has made the grab miss. Your block is a good form of insurance in case he sees your step and tries to swing his arm.

Even as your left hand strikes his arm, take it straight up and into his face, flicking him lightly across the eyes to produce a reflexive turn-away (*fig 136*). Don't withdraw your arm after the block and before striking since this wastes too much time. Your attack must follow the block as quickly as possible.

Now it may be that you get caught each time by your partner's advance and can't seem to get out of the way in time. If this happens don't worry. It takes time for true reflex responses to develop.

Start the second sequence of this section with the same opening positions. The attacker steps forward and once again tries to grasp your lapel. Step to the side as before and slap the arm away but this time leave the blocking hand in light contact with the attacker, using your right hand to attack his face with either palm-heel or claw-hand (*fig 137*). If you have not turned your trunk into the block, you should be able to use palm-heel without too much problem. Try and make the block and counter-attack as near simultaneous as possible and avoid a 'one-pause-two' operation. Try also to hit the attacker before he has stopped moving forwards and regained the initiative.

Both of these techniques work best if you sidestep just sufficiently to make the grab miss. This leaves you close enough to reach the attacker's face without either leaning precariously, or twisting your body. If you find yourself further away, it may be as well to use a kick as in the third sequence.

Fig 137

Fig 138   Fig 139

This time as he step forward, draw back your front foot just sufficiently to pull your body out of range and use a downwards moving double circular block to halt the grab (*fig 138*). Even as it
makes contact, press down on your front foot and snap kick with
the right into his groin (*fig 139*). Don't go overboard with the kick
– a light flick will suffice and allow you carefully to set down the
kicking leg afterwards. An overexuberant kick can send your
weight too far forwards, causing you to fall into the arms of the
attacker. Do not lean forward with your face as you kick, just in
case the attacker decides to try a last-ditch punch.

Range the technique correctly, adjusting the extent of your step-
back with the length of his advance. If he is covering a lot of
ground, slide back first with the rear foot, then with the front. The
important thing is to block him well out from your body – don't
let him succeed in catching hold.

The fourth technique uses an upwards rising double circular
block to lift an incoming arm up and to the side. Start from the
same stances as previously described and as the attacker comes
forward, bring your weight back over your rear leg. Block well out
from your body, trapping the lunging front arm on your crossed
forearms (*fig 140*) and lifting it up and out of the line of your body
with your left arm (*fig 141*). This phase of the block lays the foun-
dations for a powerful elbow strike with the right arm (*fig 142*).
If the attacker is much taller than you are, then use an upwards-
travelling elbow block to the point of his jaw.

The attacker generates a lot of energy as he barrels into you and the circular block is nothing if not an efficient means of energy redirection. Do not be surprised therefore if the block unbalances and sends him toppling diagonally forwards. Under those circumstances, a follow-up strike is unnecessary. If he succeeds in keeping his balance, hit him with elbow strike even as your block is in progress. Don't give him time to work out what you are doing.

140

141

Fig 142

Fig 143

Fig 144

The fifth technique features a knee-strike to the attacker's groin. Be careful when practising this because he can fall forwards after the block, moving onto the rising knee with painful results! Everything is as before except that the rising double circular block now takes the attacker's arm out on your right forearm (*fig 143*). This closes you off completely from a second grab or punch whilst opening the attacker to the knee-strike (*fig 144*). Pull clear once you have hit him but do not assume he is finished and relax your attention.

Next comes the use of grappling techniques to secure the attacker's limbs and as in the series listed above, there are five to learn. They are more difficult to use than impact techniques and require much practice to set up the necessary mental linkages so each can be performed smoothly and quickly. Here more than in the impact techniques it is necessary to keep the attacker on the move and confused because the counter takes longer to apply. Having said all that, the responses suggested here have all been tried in situations of actual combat and do work.

Begin from the same stance as before and as the attacker lunges forwards, side-step and turn with him, slapping his right hand off target (*fig 145*). Keep your left hand in contact with his wrist as you block and grasp it firmly. Continue turning and as you do so, draw the attacker's arm out straight. There should be no resistance to this, since you are merely helping him to go the way he was moving in the first place.

Fig 145

Fig 146

Fig 147

Fig 148

As you turn, smoothly rotate his wrist so his little finger is turned uppermost. By now his arm will have straightened across your chest and your left forearm is exactly overlying it (*fig 146*). Trap it so your left arm can't inadvertently slip off by bringing your right arm up and under his forearm, holding it firmly against you (*fig 147*). Continue pulling him forwards and rotating your body until his arm is fully extended and painfully immobilised (*fig 148*).

Fig 149   Fig 150

The name of the technique is 'Wrist-trap' and by skilful usage, the attacker can be brought to his knees and held there. The next technique is named 'Wrist-turn' and uses the same opening attack deflected with a slapping block. The blocking hand seizes the attacker's wrist in an over-arm grasp (*fig 149*) and the right hand is then brought around to reinforce it (*fig 150*). Notice how the thumbs are crossed in the centre-line of the attacker's hand.

As the grip is reinforced, step right around with the front foot and strongly twist your hips. As you are turning thus, apply pressure to the back of the attacker's wrist, directing it so it follows the way the trapped fingers are pointing (*fig 151*). Do not try to twist the attacker's wrist outwards and don't let your elbows rise and move out from your own mid-line. If this causes insufficient pain to the erstwhile attacker, slide your right fingers up and over his, using the palm of your hand in this manner to apply extra leverage (*fig 152*).

As with the previous technique, this hold must be applied whilst you are both moving.

The arm-entangle is a fluid hold that quickly follows a downwards travelling double circular block. As the attacker lunges forwards, move back onto your rear leg. If his advance covers a lot of ground, step back with the right, then the left leg. The greater the force of his attack, the more he is redirected downwards and

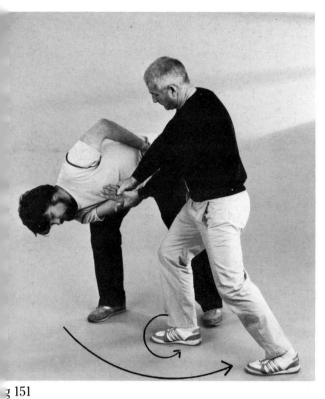

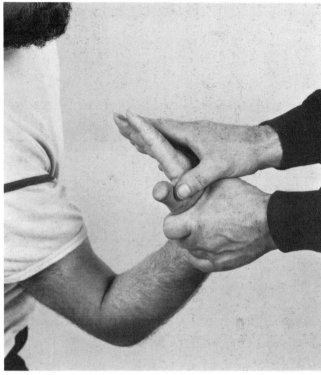

Fig 151

Fig 152

to the side (*fig 153*). Your left arm loops under his and traps his elbow joint between your bicep and forearm whilst your right arm reaches forwards and takes his shoulder (*fig 154*). Lift your left arm, keeping it tight to your chest whilst pressing down with the right, so you straighten up and bring him close into your thigh (*fig 155*). The lock applies pressure to his elbow joint, locking it out straight.

Fig 153

Fig 154

Fig 155

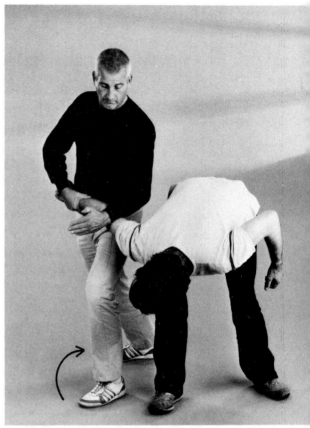

Fig 156   Fig 157

Arm-twist makes use of an upwards-travelling double circular block in response to the customary attack. The attacking arm is taken up and out on the right forearm (*fig 156*) and his wrist is grasped tightly and painfully twisted as the block continues to travel on its downwards sector. Turn your hips and move in close to the attacker as you press down on his extended right elbow with your forearm (*fig 157*). Apply force directly downwards and don't let the trapped arm move away from the front of your thighs.

Arm-turn reverses the direction of the attack, turning it back on itself. Ordinarily this would not seem a logical thing to do but arm-turn focuses on the elbow joint, folding it in its normal direction of movement and taking the attacker over backwards.

Use the familiar attack whilst stepping back slightly to maintain a safe distance. Catch the incoming arm on a downwards-travelling double circular block and take hold of his wrist with your right arm. Draw him forwards a short distance in the direction he was moving, so his balance is disturbed and then suddenly switch direction, moving his arm upwards and back towards him so his elbow is forced to bend (*fig 158*). Step into him and note

158

Fig 159

how his wrist is held in a bent position as your left arm slips behind his forearm. Extend your left hand and stiffen the fingers whilst forcing the edge against his bent wrist (*fig 159*)

Practising these wrist holds for the first time will lead to painful joints so we recommend you take it easy for the first few training sessions. If the lock becomes painful, slap your partner's back or thigh in the process known as 'Tapping up'. If you can't find a bit of him to tap, slap your own thigh or thump the mat. It is not clever to delay releasing your partner when he/she has tapped up since joint injuries are easily caused.

15
Working at Close Range

In the previous section we considered ten techniques which can be applied when the opponent is at a distance. In this section, we will look at another module of ten techniques to use when distance has been closed. In this latter situation there is less room for manoeuvre so the response has got to be made quickly and effectively – there is no second try!

As in the previous section, a cooperative partner is essential to the learning process. He must not oblige you by falling over unless your throw has actually succeeded. If it has not, then re-examine your technique with reference to the description and photographs. Your partner will not thank you for dumping him hard onto the ground after each throw and we suggest that you satisfy yourself only that his balance has been broken. Your partner should not resist the throw because it is difficult enough to learn as it is.

You are going to spend some time pulling on each other's clothes and rolling about on the floor. Therefore wear old clothes that you don't mind getting ripped or dirtied. Though you can wear tracksuits or martial arts suits for practising, there is much to be said for training in the type of clothes you generally wear.

The first technique uses a lunging movement to topple your opponent diagonally over his rear foot. Stand with your left foot forwards as the opponent grabs your left lapel with his right hand. Immediately respond by grasping his elbow with your left hand and the collar of his jacket with your right (*fig 160*). Pull down and back with your left arm, lower your head and lunge forwards, bringing your right foot forward and to the outside of his (*fig 161*). Hook back into his supporting leg as you topple him diagonally over it.

Remember to keep your head low as you lunge or he can turn the tables on you. This throw depends upon firmly controlling his upper body so a good grip is essential. Use any incidental motion to help and if he drags you towards him, resist for an instant and then complement his pull with a strong push. Alternatively, try and pull away from his grasp, so he is forced to pull you – then go for it.

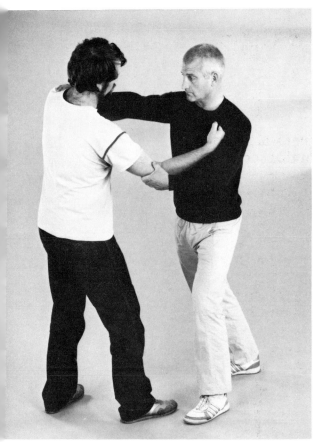

Fig 161

Fig 160

'Leg-sweep' is a similar technique and also relies upon taking his point of balance beyond his rear foot. Take up the same grip on his arm and collar and again pull down on his right elbow whilst pushing back with your right hand. This tilts and twists his upper body backwards, making his balance precarious. Lower your head, step slightly forwards and to the outside with your right foot to give yourself stability and sweep around with your left leg (*fig 162*). Strike into the back of his right leg with your lower calf muscle, trapping it as he falls backwards.

You must make his stance unstable in the first instance or the leg-sweep will not be sufficiently strong to unbalance him. Use your arms to put him into the position where he is most susceptible to loss of balance and if necessary, provoke him into jerking you forwards. Use the full weight of your leg during the sweep, pivotting on the supporting foot and allowing your hips to rotate fully into the sweep. Don't let your foot lift high off the ground. It just skims over the surface and catches him just above the heel.

Fig 162

The third technique of this series is called 'Body drop'. It is a throwing technique used from the same sort of position as we have seen above. The opponent takes your lapel in his right hand and you respond by grasping his elbow with your left hand and holding his lapel with your right (*fig 163*). Your left leg swings around and behind the right as you pull down on his elbow and push up against his lapel. As you do this, you will wind into the opponent's body and if you drop your knees during the turn, you will go under his centre of gravity.

Continue the turn until your back is to the opponent, taking a small step out with your right leg so it comes to lie outside of his right foot. Keep your hands firmly clamped to his jacket (*fig 164*). Pull down with the left hand whilst pushing up with the right and lever him over your right leg.

Like all throws, the movement must be powerful and smooth. Take control of the opponent through your grip on his jacket and don't let go. As you become more used to the technique, you will find you can spin around, drop and step out with the right foot quite quickly enough to throw an unsuspecting opponent.

It is not necessary to dump your partner on the floor with each throw. Once you have spun into position, lever him up and around and he can skip over your right foot.

 163

Fig 164

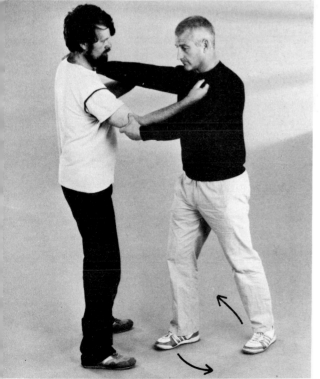

'Hip-throw' is a similar technique starting from the same position except that you release the opponent's left lapel and loop your right hand over his shoulder so the elbow lodges around his neck (*fig 165*). This time as you spin, bring your feet together and lower your body (*fig 166*). Just before the throw is executed, your back is turned fully to the opponent, his right arm is firmly pinioned and your knees are well bent. Lever him onto your hip (*fig 167*) and topple him forwards onto his back in front of you.

Fig 165

Fig 166

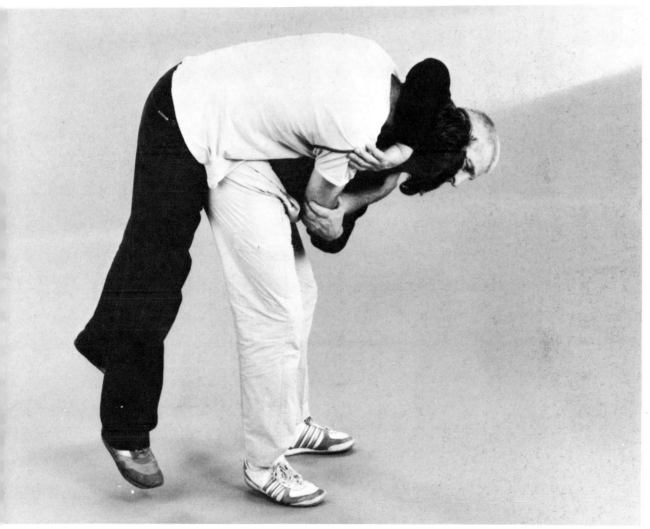

167

'Shoulder-throw' is again very similar to the foregoing except that now your right hand stays close to your chest and as you spin around, it slides under the opponent's trapped right arm and helps move him up and over (*fig 168*). As before, keep your feet close together and bend your knees.

The preceding throws can be performed when both partners are a little way apart because the spinning movement that begins them closes distance effectively. The next five techniques however are used when both parties have closed still further and all the heaving about has tipped both onto the ground. Many fight situations degenerate into wrestling about on the floor so it is as well to know what that entails.

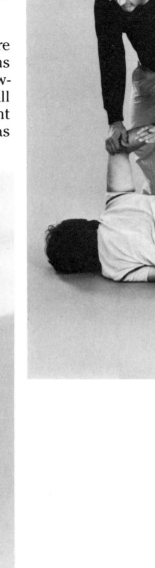

Fig 168

 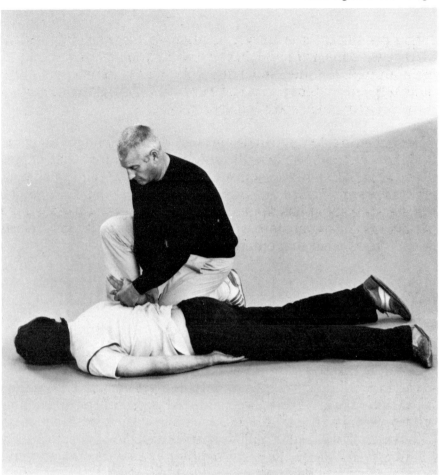

Fig 169   Fig 170

High-power strikes are out because you are both too close and unable to use your body properly to accelerate them. Lower powered strikes to vulnerable areas are still possible though you may not be at your most accurate. This is when the principles of leverage and areas of vulnerability assume great importance.

Your partner lies on his back and offers his right arm. You stand on his left side and take the wrist of his outstretched arm with your left hand. Sharply pull him towards you and bend his wrist into a gooseneck hold. Take his straightened elbow with your right hand and press down on it, so he is forced onto his face (*fig 169*). Quickly kneel down close to his side and bring the trapped wrist down and around, controlling his elbow with your right hand. Stop the movement when the painfully bent wrist comes to lie near his shoulderblade (*fig 170*). This technique is called 'Wrist-lock'.

The second of these techniques is called 'Arm-entangle' and it follows the same principles as the similarly named technique in the previous section. From a kneeling position at the opponent's right side, take his right wrist and draw it out straight. At the same time rotate it firmly whilst pressing down on his extended elbow joint with the edge of your left hand (*fig 171*). Bring his arm around, using your left hand to control the elbow (*fig 172*). Lock his wrist in the crook of your left elbow and press against his upper arm. Release the wrist-hold and use your right hand to push him firmly into the ground, so he is unable to pull away (*fig 173*).

Fig 171

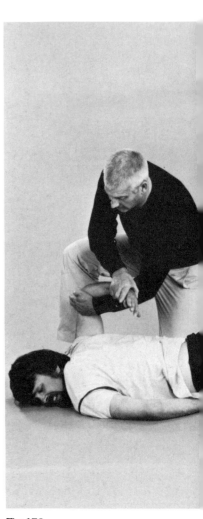

Fig 172

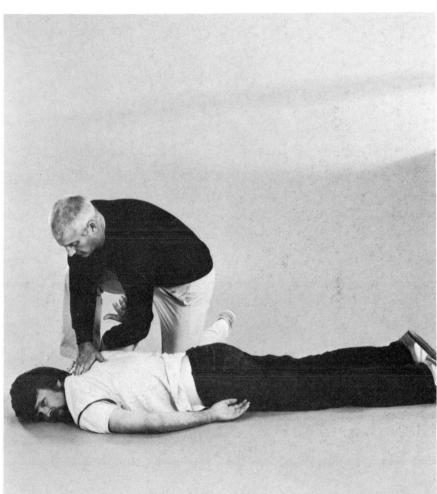

Fig 173

Fig 174

Fig 175

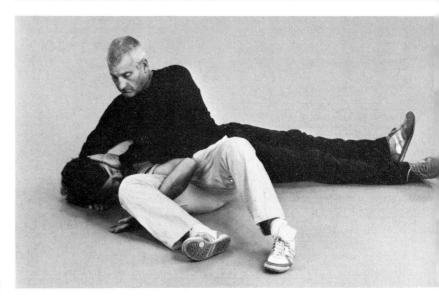

Fig 176

The third technique is called 'Cross-hold'. Have your partner lie on his back and approach him from his right. Lie across his chest with the right side of your body and force your right arm under his neck, seizing his collar or lapel in your right hand. Spread your legs wide to provide stability and take his right wrist with your left hand. Turn his forearm so the palm of his hand faces your face and push it back until the elbow straightens against your thigh (*fig 174*).

Bend his elbow as you hook your right leg back and over the top of his wrist (*fig 175*). By varying the pressure applied by your right knee, you can inflict pain on his right elbow and shoulder joint. Press down over his face with your left hand, forcing his head to turn to the side (*fig 176*). This will prevent the possibility of a head butt. Do not block off his air passage.

Necklock is a firm way of holding someone immobile whilst help is summoned. Your partner lies on his back and extends his right arm upwards. Drop onto your right knee close by his right hip and push his arm away from you with your left hand. At the same time, reach down to the left side of his neck with your right arm (*fig 177*). Drop your weight down onto your right elbow and force your arm under the back of his neck. His right arm is trapped across the side of his own jaw and away from mischief. Slide your left hand down and interlace fingers with your right arm. Bring your head close to your partner's and hold him firmly (*fig 178*). Keep your feet widely splayed for stability.

g 177

Fig 178

The fifth technique is 'Folding wrist-lock', taking the partner's right wrist with your right arm as you approach from his right side. Sit down abruptly, wedging your right shin against his side and swinging your left leg across his neck and lower face. Reinforce your hold on his wrist with your left hand and apply a gooseneck lock (*fig 179*). When the lock is on, slide your left hand around to the back of his hand and use this to apply additional pressure. His right elbow is jammed against your thigh (*fig 180*) and leverage can be increased by sliding your grip down towards his knuckles.

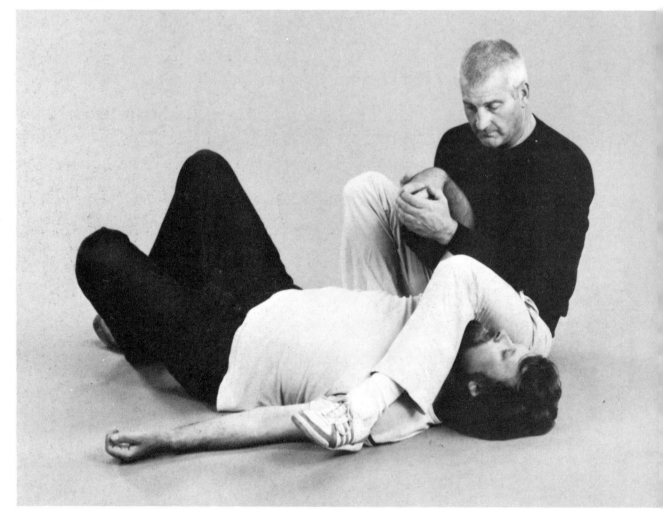

Fig 179

Fig 180

16

Combining Techniques Together

A lucky snap kick that catches the attacker's groin, or a flick of the fingers which lightly touches the cornea of the eye can provide sufficient opportunity for you to escape without the need to do anything more than run away. Unfortunately you can't count on this happening during an attack and it is as well if you have a secondary technique that can be quickly brought into play.

This secondary technique can be a strike, kick, throw or hold applied under the cover afforded by the opening response. To have its best effect, it must be applied before the opponent has fully recovered from the effects of your first response.

The secondary technique must follow in a logical way, extending and harmonising with the movements you made in the first instance. This allows it to follow quickly, without the need for a sudden changing of direction and stance. The attacker will not remain still after your first response and any secondary technique application must take this into account. Get your partner to respond realistically – as though the first technique had been properly applied. This will allow you to gauge the application of the second.

We recommend that you study the three sets of three combinations we have set out for you since they will serve as a basic introduction to technique linking. When you can perform them quickly and smoothly, try making up some of your own by intermixing from the techniques given in the two preceding sections. As a rule of thumb, always distract with a fast striking technique before you try to apply a hold.

The first combination of the first set uses a straightforward slapping block followed by a flick to the eyes. Begin from left defensive posture and take up a suitable distance and line. The attacker must not be able to reach you without first stepping forwards. As he comes forward onto his right foot, he reaches forward with his right hand as though to take your lapel. Take a sizeable step to his closed side and deflect his arm with your left hand (*fig 181*). Follow this with a finger-flick to his eyes (*fig 182*) and as he pulls his head away, use your right foot to kick him forcefully in the groin (*fig 183*). The kick you are using works best from a fair distance so make sure you step wide of him as he comes forward.

181

Fig 182

Fig 183

The second combination of the first set uses the same opening format except that after the flick to his eyes, quickly seize his outstretched arm with your right before it can be withdrawn. Step up with your right foot to get your positioning correct and then use your left in a swing into the rear of his right leg, knocking it diagonally forwards and therebye breaking his balance (*fig 184*).

This technique will not work unless you position yourself correctly before using the sweep. You must be well balanced and in range to make the leg-sweep effective. Do not strike him to the side of his ankle but curl around behind his foot, knocking it the way it is facing. Do not release your grip on his right arm.

Fig 184

The third technique of the first set again uses a slap block followed by a finger-flick to the eyes. As you make the flick, seize his outstretched wrist with your right hand. Bend it into a gooseneck and take it back and towards his face as you advance on your left leg. Bring your left arm around his forearm, looping it through so the little finger-edge presses into his wrist in the hold known as 'Arm turn' (*fig 185*). Force him to lean back and throw your head forward whilst hooking your right leg behind his in a leg-trip (*fig 186*).

g 185

Fig 186

Fig 187   Fig 188

The fourth sequence and first of the second set uses a down-wards-travelling circular block to take the opponent's right hand down and to the left side. Range the block by either pulling your weight back over the rear leg or by taking a short step backwards. Block well out from your body and as his lunge is coming to a stop, snap kick into his groin off your right leg (*fig 187*). Keep your left arm in contact with his and drop your weight forwards, delivering a swinging elbow strike on landing (*fig 188*). Use the energy of your moving body to inject extra power into the strike. If your block has deflected his arm downwards, use a descending elbow strike to the back of his neck (*fig 189*).

Fig 189

Fig 1[

The second technique of the second set again uses a down-wards-circling block and as you move back, catch his right wrist on your left forearm, taking it out to the side. As this is happening, snap-kick into his groin with your right foot (*fig 190*), afterwards setting it down in a forward position. Take his right shoulder

with your right arm and slide your left under his elbow, raising his forearm and applying pressure to his elbow joint by means of an arm entangle hold (*fig 191*). Don't allow him to pull away from you.

The third technique of the second set operates in exactly the same way as the preceding ones with a downwards-circling block followed by a snap kick to the opponent's groin with your right leg. Keep your left arm in contact with the opponent's right wrist and as you deliver the kick, seize his wrist strongly to prevent it from being jerked from your grasp. Drop your kicking foot to the ground and quickly step right around with your left foot, at the same time reinforcing your hold on his wrist with your right hand (*fig 192*) as you apply wrist-turn.

Fig

The first sequence of the third and final set uses an upwards-circling block that takes the attacking arm up and out on the left forearm. In this instance you have not stepped back quite so far, or perhaps you misjudged the length of your opponent's advance. Whichever is the case, you don't have the distance for a kick so as your right arm comes free, drive it into his face as a fast but low energy palm-heel or claw-hand (*fig 193*). Use this to distract as you grab the back of his neck or shoulder and pull him onto a knee to the groin (*fig 194*).

193

Fig 194

The second sequence of the third set begins in the same way with an upwards-circular block that takes the attacking arm out on your left forearm. As in the previous sequence this opens him to a fast but low energy palm-heel or claw-hand strike to the face. Use this distraction to advance with your right foot, whilst at the same time taking his left arm out to the side (*fig 195*). Throw your bodyweight forward and apply leg-trip (*fig 196*).

The third sequence of the final set opens with upwards-circular block and a palm-heel or claw-hand to the face. The opponent's right wrist is then quickly seized with your own right hand as you withdraw it after the opening strike (*fig 197*). Lift his arm and step under it, swinging around with your right leg and forcing his wrist into a gooseneck hold (*fig 198*). Bring your left hand up and press down on his elbow, forcing his head down and holding him with arm-twist (*fig 199*).

Fig 195

Fig 196

197

Fig 198

Fig 199

17

Escape Techniques

Escape techniques is the name given to a class of responses to use when the opponent has actually got a grip of you. Distance and line are now no longer involved and your whole body movement is reduced. In such situations, just think to yourself "What weapons have I got free?" and "What targets are exposed?" Put the two answers together and you have the beginnings of an escape technique.

In some cases you have very little time to respond. If your opponent's strangle is applied correctly you will have barely enough time to make one decisive response before total panic sets in, quickly followed by unconsciousness. Can you see a target? Is one near at hand?

Some of the holds your partner applies will be potentially painful so ensure he knows what is expected of him. Whilst you are learning the escape, your attacker should always show restraint, varying the force he uses in relation to your improving ability. Don't be kind to yourself when practising because it is important to learn how to cope with a realistic attack. Additionally, certain protocols must be followed. The first is that the attacker must respond as though you had delivered a technique correctly.

Quite often a student will come to the training session and complain that they tried the technique with a friend from outside the club and though the escape was meticulously performed, they just couldn't seem to break free. When you ask them if they applied the opening strike to the groin at full power, they say "Of course not!" and there is the cause of the failure. Only a highly skilled person can apply a technique directly and without the benefit of a distraction.

The corollary of this is that you shouldn't keep dumping your partner hard on the floor because sooner or later he is going to get bruised. It is far better to take a throw to the point of imbalance – feel him teetering over – and then allow him to regain his balance perhaps by jumping around you.

Fig 200

The second protocol to observe is that although your partner knows what is coming next, he must not alter his attack. For example, if he knows that you are going to block his arm in a certain direction, he may mis-direct it on purpose to minimise his otherwise bruised wrist.

In this section we have assembled five fairly common attacking holds and suggested alternative responses to each. The attacks are shown correctly applied – for there is a tendency in some schools of self defence to alter the attack so it is amenable to a particular response. This of course, is a bad idea and will not equip you to deal with an actual attack.

The first escape is from a side head-lock. To apply this technique, the opponent stands to one side and wraps his stronger arm around your head. He pulls your head down until it is held firm against his hip where he can apply painful pressure to your neck and face. Left to his own devices, he will probably use this hold to drag you off somewhere, or he may decide either to bash your head into a wall or to punch you in the face.

React quickly by punching him in the groin with your right fist (*fig 200*). This will break his concentration and may cause him to loosen his grip. Seize the front of his right thigh with your right hand and bar your left arm across his face. Pull up with your right hand whilst pushing his head backwards (*fig 201*). If he turns his hips away from you, you can still attack the flesh on the inside of his thigh. Grasp it firmly between index finger and thumb and twist it until he releases.

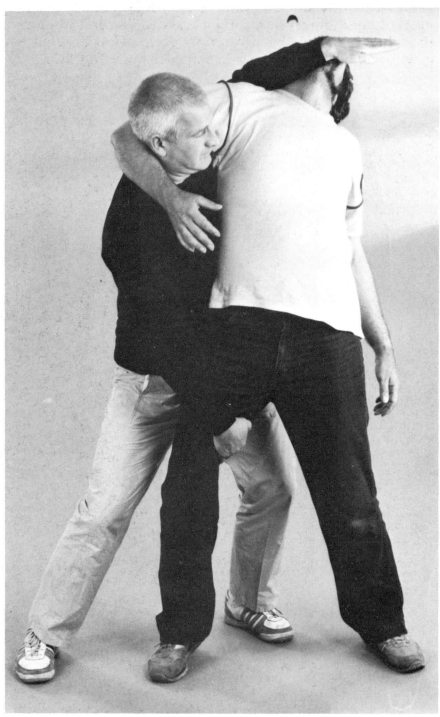

Fig 201

Next try an escape from rear strangle. Your partner stands close behind and whips his right arm around your throat, locking the hold with his left hand. Think which weapons you have free and what targets you can go for and the escape becomes obvious. Move your hip slightly to the right and bring your left hammer fist back sharply into his groin (*fig 202*). Follow this by reaching for his upper arm with your right hand and grabbing him near the elbow with your left. Drop right down below his centre of gravity and unbalance him with shoulder-throw (*fig 203*).

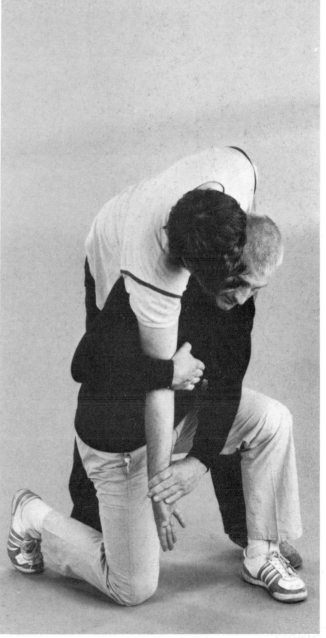

g 202

Fig 203

A front bear hug can be extremely painful but since it leaves both of your hands free and his face obligingly near by, it is not difficult to escape from. Get him to release by either pressing on his closed eyes, or by attacking just under the point of his jaw with a one-knuckle fist (*fig 204*). As soon as you have freedom to move, whip your right arm smartly around the back of his neck, seize his right arm with your left and twist your body around whilst bringing your feet together and bending your knees (*fig 205*). Lever him up and over with a hip-throw.

Fig 204

Fig 205

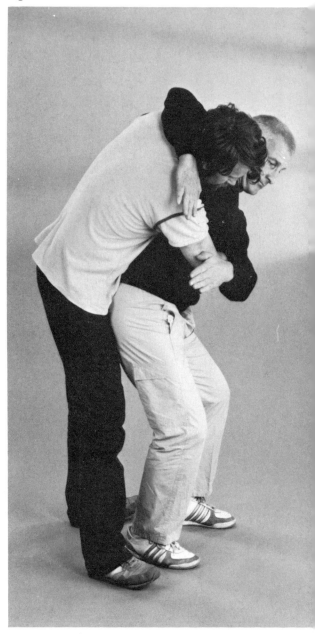

A rear bear hug pinions both arms above the elbows and is a little more difficult to deal with. Move your hip slightly to the right and strike back with left hammer-fist into his groin. It matters not that the strike has little power, because even a light impact will loosen the grip and allow you to seize his right wrist with your left (*fig 206*). Pull down on and twist his right arm as your own right hand drives up against his upper arm for shoulder-throw. As you are about to do this, drop right down and topple him over you (*fig 207*).

Fig 206

Fig 207

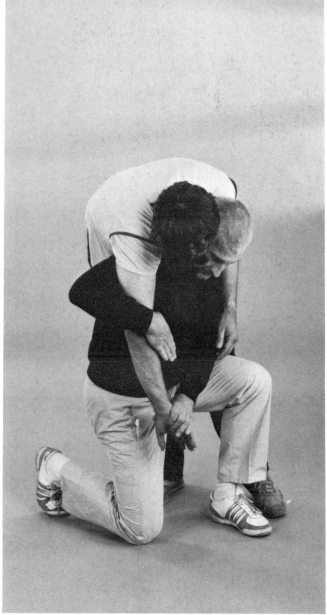

One-handed lapel grabs are dangerous because they hold you firmly for a following punch. Although these escape techniques work from either side with only the smallest modification, for the sake of practice assume that the opponent is right handed and grabs you with his left hand prior to a right punch. Stand in left posture and respond as soon as the grab is made by making a fast attack with your left hand to the opponent's eyes. This creates a momentary distraction during which time you can seize the opponent's left wrist with your right hand and turning away, stretch his arm out with your forearm overlying it, into a wrist-trap hold (*fig 208*). Reinforce the hold with your left hand.

The second response to a one-handed lapel grab uses a palm-heel strike with your left hand to the chin or nose, driving the attacker's head backwards (*fig 209*). Immediately range yourself by positioning your left leg and leg sweep his left leg with your right. Control him by taking his left elbow with your right hand and pushing with your left palm against his left shoulder (*fig 210*).

Fig

Fig 209

Fig

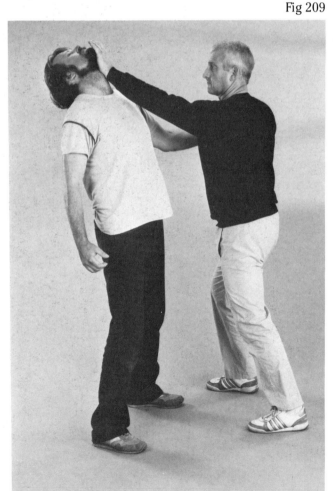

A double-handed lapel grab means that your opponent can attack you with only his knees or head. Extend the fingers of your right hand and push them into the base of his throat (*fig 211*). This has the effect of forcing his head back whilst you take a firm hold of his right elbow with your left hand. Now take his lapel with your right. Spin around sharply and step to the outside of his right leg with your right (*fig 212*), then lever him over with a body-drop.

g 211   Fig 212

The second counter to a double-handed lapel grab uses an inside leg-sweep. Start as before, the opponent taking your lapels in a firm grip. Move slightly forward on your right leg and push the stiffened fingers of your right hand into the base of his throat, forcing his upper body to lean back from you. Take his right elbow with your left hand at the same time (*fig 213*). Bring your left leg up a little way and then drive your right through and hook against his right leg with your heel so he falls backwards (*fig 214*). The continuing strong push into the base of his throat forces his centre of gravity beyond his back leg, making him vulnerable.

Fig 213

Fig 214

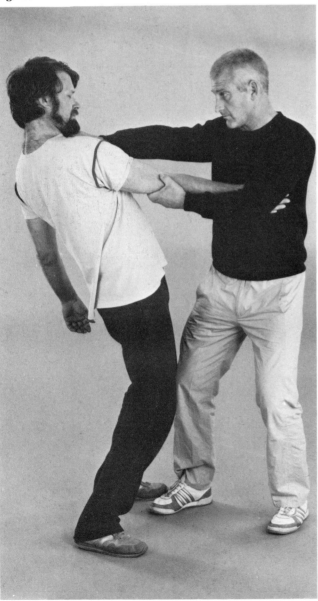

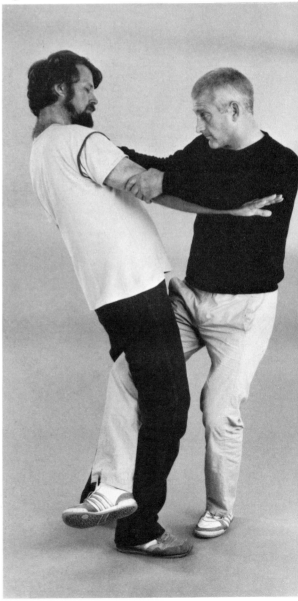

The final pair of escape techniques operate from a prone position. Lie on your back and your opponent kneels astride and presses down on you. Your arms are pinioned to either side of your head (*fig 215*). First gather your knees up and then relax all your muscles prior to driving your left arm out to the side. If this is sudden enough, it will take the opponent's weight diagonally forwards. As this happens, violently twist your body to the left and throw him off (*fig 216*). Force up your right hand at the same time to get additional purchase.

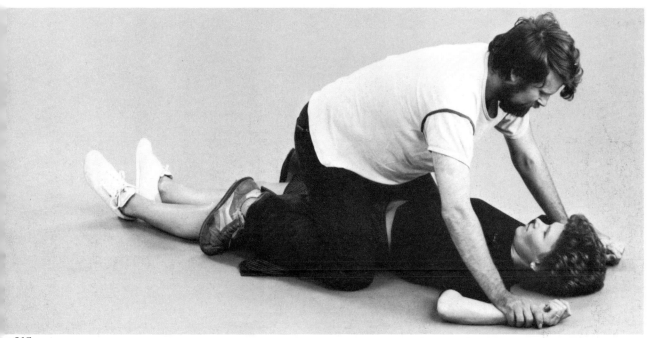

g 215

Fig 216

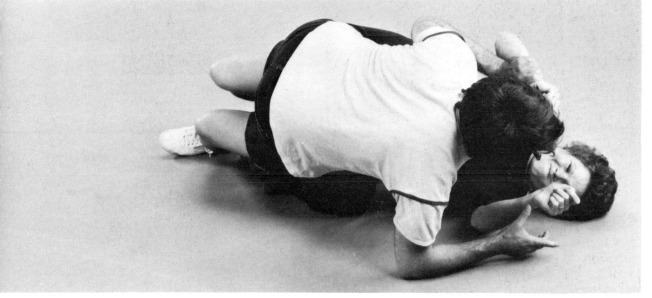

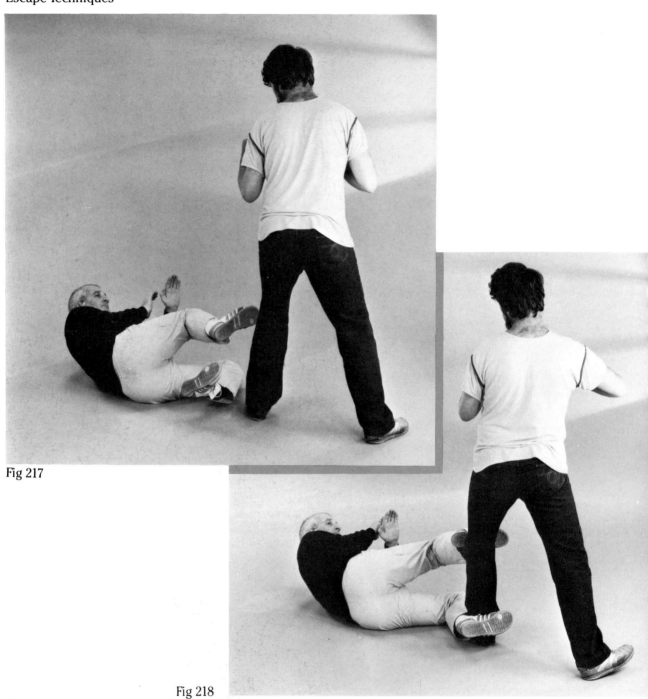

Fig 217

Fig 218

In the last situation, you have fallen to the ground but your opponent has not and may kick you at any time. Keep your arms close to your body and use one leg to paddle yourself around so your feet are always towards him (*fig 217*). When he comes close enough, lash out at his groin and if the opportunity presents itself, hook his ankle whilst kicking his knee (*fig 218*). As an alternative, fling yourself into his shins, trapping his feet as you push him backwards (*fig 219*). Roll up and over his legs as he falls back and strike him in the groin or face with a hammer-fist (*fig 220*).

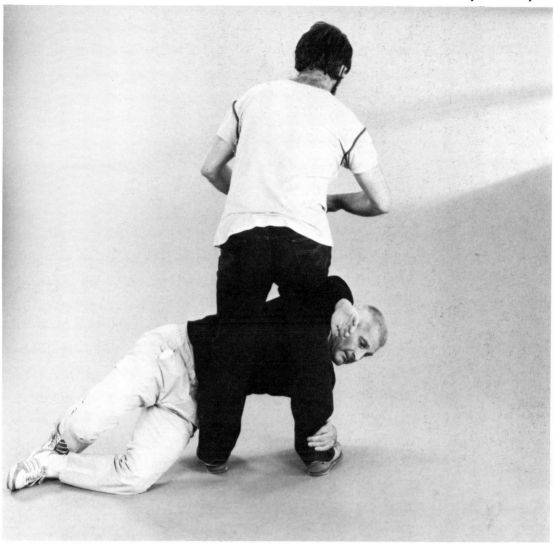

Fig 219

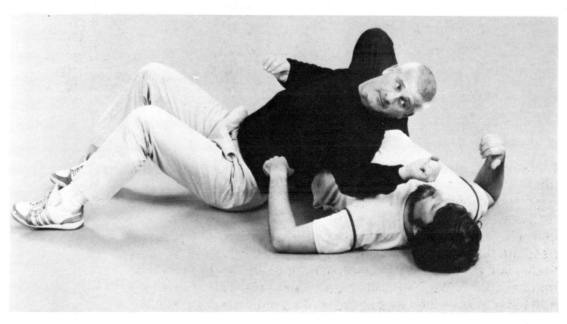

Fig 220

18
Weapons and Self Defence

In any situation there may be weapons of opportunity to hand if you look around. Striking weapons must have enough mass to inflict a sizeable impact yet be short enough to manoeuvre in the space available. They must be quickly reversible; that is to say, you must be able to quickly switch from one direction to another with them. Use striking weapons not only to swing at a target with but also to extend the length of your arm. A swing is easily seen and avoided whilst a jab is not.

Don't carry a knife in your leading hand. Hold it back against your body and slash quickly with it. Aim to cut the limbs rather than the face or body. Do not pick up a knife unless you are prepared to use it!

There is no defence against a firearm unless the user is stupid enough to move into your effective range. Even then do consider that it takes less time to pull a trigger than it does to strike at someone's eyes or groin.

If the attacker has a baton, watch distance and line carefully. A lot of recovery time follows a wild swing and that is the safest time to bounce in and counter-attack. If the attacker pulls a knife, slip your jacket or coat around your forearm to act as a shield. If you aren't wearing either, pull your shoe off and put that over your hand. Keep well away from the attacker and wait for him to over-extend. If you must hack at him, use your feet and keep your body back from danger.

For obvious safety reasons your partner must use a rubber knife during practice. Unfortunately this will not prepare you for the frightening sight of a real one, where one slip-up will be painful, if not fatal. Use a lightweight stick for the baton and a walking stick for the staff. The lighter the weapon, the less bruised you will both be at the end of training though such safety weapons do not give the correct feel. Compensate by doing some solitary practice with real weapons. Face yourself in a full length mirror and look for openings as you slash, stab and parry.

Moving on to the practical employment of these ideas, let's begin with defence against a truncheon. If the attacker is not an expert in weapons usage, he will swing the truncheon at its target to inflict damage. In the first instance he will aim at the head or neck.

Face your armed opponent in left posture and watch for his movement. The truncheon must travel a fair distance so you have enough time to respond. Either stand your ground or move into the opponent as he advances, bringing your hands up in a double-handed circling block. Reach out for his descending wrist and as it meets yours, snap kick off your right leg (*fig 221*), then seize and twist his wrist with your right hand. Bring your right leg quickly around and push down on his elbow with your left forearm, applying a firm arm-twist (*fig 222*).

The movement is fluid with no delay between the block, the snap-kick and arm-twist. If you have stepped into his attack, you may find that you are too close to kick, so use your knee instead.

Step in also to a downwards/diagonal strike. Move your right foot forwards and diagonally out to the right as you go to meet the strike. Turning your hips slightly, take the descending blow on your wrists (*fig 223*) but this time seize his wrist with your left hand, allowing the blow to follow through. Draw up your left leg and push hard at his left shoulder with your right hand whilst sweeping his left leg with your right foot (*fig 224*). Control him through the wrist and shoulder holds and watch out for wildly swinging arms.

Fig 223   Fig 224

ig 222

The next two responses are made against a knife-wielding attacker and and it is worth re-emphasising that no response at all should be attempted unless you are certain that to do nothing places you in greater danger. The attacker may try to grab you with his left hand but forget the hand on your lapel and go for the knife hand instead. Grab it with both hands interlacing your thumbs on the back of his hand (*fig 225*) and step violently round whilst applying a powerful wrist-turn. Keep his arm close to your body. As the pressure on his wrist increases, his grip on your lapel loosens and you can turn fully into the full lock position (*fig 226*).

In the second sequence, you have succeeded in bundling your raincoat or jacket over your right forearm so use it as a flail to strike him across the face (*fig 227*). As part of the same movement, bring your right foot up in a snap kick to his groin (*fig 228*). The movement must be as one, otherwise he will slash at your leg or groin.

Fig 225

Fig 226

Fig 228

g 227

139

In the next section, you have armed yourself with a short baton such as a pastry roller or heavy torch. Although this theoretically improves your chances, the attacker still has the advantage. As he advances to slash at you, move diagonally forward and to the right. Aim a slashing blow at his wrist (*fig 229*) and snap-kick him in the groin. Now comes the fancy bit. Land forward from the kick and catch his right wrist on your left forearm but be careful of that knife. Lift the baton to the top of his arm (*fig 230*).

Step around to his side with your right leg and bring your left hand up so it seizes the other end of the baton just above his elbow. His right wrist is now trapped in the crook of your left elbow. Press down hard on his right elbow as you continue stepping around (*fig 231*) and apply arm-entangle.

Fig 229

Fig 230

Fig 2

Arm-entangle is used again in the next response because it is a good lock for use in conjunction with the baton. This time your opponent is unarmed and steps forward to take a swing at your face with his right hand. Hold either end of the baton and twist your forearms towards the incoming punch (*fig 232*). Advance diagonally to the right with your right leg and immediately the

Fig 23?

swing is blocked, release your left grip and swing the baton around, cracking him in the knee, ribs (*fig 233*) or jaw. Pass the baton between his left arm and ribs whilst closing against his left side. Bring the baton up and seize the other end of it before pulling it down against his elbow. His wrist is caught on your right forearm (*fig 234*).

Fig 233

Fig 234

The next technique is effective against kicks, using the baton as a hard bar against which the attacker's shin collides. Hold both ends of the baton as in the previous response and as the attacker kicks, jump forwards and jam the baton down onto his rising shin (*fig 235*). Don't lean your face forward and hold the baton tightly to avoid having it jarred from your hands. Withdraw the baton and transfer weight onto your back leg before driving it double-handed back into his chest or chin (*fig 236*). Put a lot of body-weight behind the strike.

Fig 235

A longer baton – such as an umbrella – can be used to jab the opponent hard where it hurts. The baton is hard and has a narrow cross-section so impact is concentrated over a very small area. In the following sequence, a longer baton (or 'staff') is used firstly in this manner and then to apply the by now familiar arm-entangle.

Fig 236

As the attacker moves towards you, crack him hard across the thigh with the staff and then change to a double-hand grip with the right hand near the base and the left half way along. Lunge forwards and dig the staff hard into his floating ribs (*fig 238*). Knock his right arm to the side and slide the staff under his right armpit (*fig 239*). Then step right around with your right foot and lever the staff upwards against his forearm (*fig 240*). Advance forwards whilst slightly lifting your right hand and you will take him face-downwards into the ground (*fig 241*).

Fig 237

Fig 238

Fig 239

Fig 240

Fig 241

If he grabs hold of the staff with both hands, snap-kick him in the groin with your right foot (*fig 242*). This will loosen his grip and allow you to step around with your right foot whilst rotating and pushing the staff. If he keeps hold, both wrists will be painfully twisted (*fig 243*).

g 242

Fig 243

The final sequence pits the staff against a swinging punch. Step back and strike the punching forearm smartly with the staff (*fig 244*), then pull it back and smack the attacker in the ribs (*fig 245*). Release your right grip on the staff and seize his right wrist, drawing his arm out and towards you (*fig 246*). Jam the staff across his right elbow and press down on it (*fig 247*) forcing him down onto his face.

Fig 244

Fig 2

Fig 246

Fig 2

19
Free Sparring

Free sparring is a form of training where the attacks and responses are not agreed in advance. Having said that, at this initial stage it is not completely free inasmuch as we suggest the attacking partner limits his or herself to standardised forms of attack that the defender has become used to during this course. Naturally this reduces the efficacy of the training itself in that you cannot expect an attacker to follow pre-agreed guidelines. On the other hand, it retains some value in that it teaches you to respond in a way that has some links with a true attack.

A word to the wise; do not begin free sparring until you have mastered the techniques contained in this book and can perform them quickly, correctly and safely.

Let's begin by looking at some general guidelines for free sparring. First of all, make sure the area you will train in is free from hazards and large enough for the purpose. A square of eight metres per side is ideal. Don't train close to furniture, french windows, glass doors or pillars. Make sure that the thumps and bumps of practice can't dislodge items on a table or shelf. It is particularly important that the floor has a degree of 'give' to it. On no account free spar on a solid floor. Open a window to allow good ventilation and make sure the floor doesn't become slippery with use.

Next look at yourself and check that your long hair is held back with an elastic band. Don't use any kind of metal hair grips and remove earrings and necklaces. These can get painfully caught. Remove all rings and those you can't remove must be covered by surgical tape. Check your fingernails to make sure they aren't ragged or dirty and if you are practising barefoot, do the same with your toenails.

Your clothes will come in for a lot of tugging and pulling so make sure they are equal to it. Judo suits are strong enough and are also light and airy. Karate suits aren't suitable. Women practitioners should wear a teeshirt under the jacket and perhaps a sports-bra to give firm support. Men are recommended to wear a groin protector using a fixed-cup design. Soft and flexible shin pads remove much of the pain from colliding shins and you can even buy ones which extend down over your instep. If you opt for the latter, choose those fashioned from an elastic tube. These are more difficult to put on and take off but they do not keep coming adrift during training as do those fastened by velcro strips.

Gumshields can be worn and it is worth noting that not only do these protect the teeth and lips but they can reduce the effects of a hard blow to the face that would otherwise result in a knock-out. If you decide to wear shoes, choose lightweight trainers or better still, the kung fu slippers you can buy in martial arts shops. Don't wear your spectacles during training. If you do, we guarantee that they will be broken sooner rather than later. Soft contact lenses are fine but keep your cleaning kit handy to deal with any that come adrift.

Match yourself as far as possible with a partner of similar size and weight. A big person is very difficult to hold or throw and your early failures will dishearten you. Perhaps even more important is the fact that large people are very powerful without knowing it. Attempts to stop even a slow and controlled punch or kick may bruise you.

Agree a training time beforehand and use a kitchen timer or a colleague with a stopwatch to signal the end of it. If you are working hard, you will find two minutes are adequate. Then have a rest for two minutes and change roles with your partner. Regulate the speed of exchanges, starting with slow attacks and as you get the hang of things, gradually speed up. Don't hurry things and don't become over-confident because that is when accidents occur. In recognition of this fact, keep a first aid kit and some kitchen towel handy.

At first the attacking partner uses only the left or the right limbs and not a mixture of both. Much later, the attacker can use a mixture of both with intent to test your true ability. Begin by facing each other from a distance of perhaps 2 metres and confirm that you are both ready. From then on the attacking partner is free to move. Stop also by an agreed signal and as you do, withdraw from each other – don't step forwards. The reason for this is that one partner may not have heard the stop signal. If he lunges forwards as you drop your guard and step forward to discuss the practice the consequences could be painful!

Stop also when you tangle up and no clear techniques develop.

Don't stop immediately you get into a grapple, in case one or other of you is able to turn it to advantage; allow perhaps ten seconds before separating by mutual consent. Allow this time to elapse even if you both go down to the floor because groundwork is an important part of self defence. You must be able to think and act in a coordinated manner from a prone position.

Don't stop straight away if the defending partner trips, or falls over. The attacker should continue for about ten seconds afterwards and try to simulate a kick in the head or body. The prone defender must try and avoid these attacks and if possible, trip the attacker. If the attacker grabs hold of you but doesn't follow with an effective technique, you should break then also.

Stop when one of you taps up – and then stop IMMEDIATELY. Stop too when one of you steps out of the area because this marks the imaginary presence of walls or fences. Give yourself a black mark each time you step out. The attacker on the other hand, will try to crowd you out by constantly closing distance and making threatening feints that encourage you to step back. By this means learn how to use an area to advantage. Try and remember the concepts of line and timing.

Free sparring becomes enjoyable when practised with two sensible partners. However in the excitement of sparring, one or both can become over-exuberant and start acting a little wildly. When this happens, you should stop immediately and withdraw from the engagement. Have a cup of tea before starting again. In this sort of situation, it is a good idea to have a third person monitor proceedings. If he/she feels things are getting out of hand, they immediately stop the match.

Using impact techniques, even when controlled, places you in danger. If your partner moves suddenly and unexpectedly you may land a hard blow which hurts either or both of you. Move quickly but do not inject a lot of power into the techniques so even if they land, they won't cause injury. Use extreme care when kicking to the groin and we recommend that you do not use the finger-flick to the eyes, or indeed any open-hand technique to the face with the exception of palm-heel.

Because the techniques are pulled in this way, your partner must honour them as though they were full-power effective strikes and react accordingly. If he was attacking as your controlled strike made light contact, then he must stop and allow you a second or so to apply a follow-up. This is most important to successful practice. Do not walk through your partner's techniques unless you believe that they missed.

The attacker will also help practice by leaving an extended arm out a little longer than would be the case in an actual fight. This facility can be gradually withdrawn as the defender's ability increases. As the corollary of this, the defender must use control when holding and throwing. The throw must be such as to allow the attacker to land safely and with minimum force.

Award yourself a point if you think that your defence has been effective. Give yourself two points if you manage to link two effective attacks such as a strike and a hold/throw. Similarly the attacker awards him or herself points for controlled strikes which land and two points if they manage a hold from which you cannot escape. A third-party can be useful for keeping tally of successful defences as against the number of attacks which got through. Try to become competitive during sparring. Remember that a good loser on the free-sparring mat will be an injured loser in the street.

For a little variation in your practice, arm the attacker with a rubber knife or light plastic baton. The attacker must only use the knife in straight thrusts but delivered with either hand. The only permissible target is the body. Whilst this is very stilted and unrealistic, it is nevertheless a safe and enjoyable way of learning free technique association.

If you get a bang on the head that makes you dizzy, stop at once and do not spar for a period of at least four weeks afterwards. You may continue to train but you should not subject your head to any further bangs or bumps.

20

The Practical Syllabus

To assist your practice we have here set out the various sections and techniques of the practical syllabus.

Preliminaries
Full warm-up exercise programme starting with whole-body exercises, going to strength/power training and concluding with a flexibility work-out.

Section 1: Working From A Distance

A: *Striking Techniques*

a) Side-step and slapping block followed by a flick to the eyes with the same hand you blocked with.

b) Side-step and slapping block followed by a claw-hand or palm-heel to the face with the other hand.

c) Step back and downwards-circling double block followed by a snap-kick into the groin.

d) Step back and upwards-circling double block followed by an elbow-strike to the point of the attacker's jaw.

e) Step back and upwards-circling double block followed by a knee-strike to the groin.

B: *Grappling Techniques*

a) Side-step and slapping block followed by wrist-trap.

b) Side-step and slapping block followed by wrist-turn.

c) Step back and downwards-circling double block followed by arm-entangle.

d) Step back and upwards-circling double block followed by arm-twist.

e) Step back and upwards-circling double block followed by arm-turn.

Section 2: Working At Close Range

A: *Standing Techniques*

a) Opponent grabs your lapel; lunge forwards and apply leg-trip.

b) Opponent grabs your lapel; lunge forwards and apply leg-sweep.

c) Opponent grabs your lapel; spin around and apply body-drop.

d) Opponent grabs your lapel; spin around and apply hip-throw.

e) Opponent grabs your lapel; spin around and apply shoulder-throw.

B: *Prone Techniques*

a) Turn prone opponent onto his face and apply wrist-lock.

b) Turn prone opponent onto his face and apply arm-entangle.

c) Lie across opponent and apply cross-hold.

d) Apply neck-lock to prone opponent.

e) Sit with leg wedged into prone opponent's back and other leg over his face. Apply folding wrist-lock.

Section 3: Combining Techniques Together

A: *First Set*

a) Side-step and slapping block followed by flick to eyes and snap-kick to groin.

b) Side-step and slapping block followed by flick to eyes and leg-sweep.

c) Side-step and slapping block followed by flick to eyes and arm-turn.

B: *Second Set*

a) Slight back-step and downwards-circling block followed by snap-kick to groin and elbow strike to chin or back of head.

b) Slight back-step and downwards-circling block followed by snap-kick to groin and arm-entangle.

c) Slight back-step and downwards-circling block followed by snap-kick to groin and wrist-turn.

C: *Third Set*

a) No back-step and upwards-circling block followed by palm-heel or claw-hand to face and knee strike to groin.

b) No back-step and upwards-circling block followed by palm-heel or claw-hand to face and leg-trip.

c) No back-step and upwards-circling block followed by palm-heel or claw-hand to face and arm-twist.

Section 4: Escape Techniques

a) Escape from side head-lock by punching the groin and levering the opponent back.

b) Escape from rear strangle by striking the opponent's groin with hammer-fist and then applying shoulder-throw.

c) Escape from front bear-hug by attacking vulnerable points on face with one-knuckle fist and then applying hip-throw.

d) Escape from rear bear-hug by striking the opponent's groin with hammer-fist and then applying shoulder-throw.

e) Escape from one-handed lapel grasp by flicking to his eyes and then applying wrist-trap.

f) Escape from one-handed lapel grasp by striking the opponent's face with claw-hand or palm-heel followed by leg-sweep.

g) Escape from a double lapel grasp by thrusting stiffened fingers into the base of the opponent's throat and following with body drop.

h) Escape from a double lapel grasp by thrusting stiffened fingers into the base of the opponent's throat and following with inside leg-sweep.

i) Escape from a prone pinion by extending your left arm and twisting your body around.

j) Take up a prone defence position and fend off his attempts to kick you. Try and trap his leg between your instep and sole of foot.

Section 5: Weapons & Self Defence

A: *You Are Unarmed*

a) Your opponent has a baton. Use upwards-circling block followed by snap-kick to groin and arm-twist.

b) Your opponent has a baton. Use upwards-circling block followed by a rapid diagonal advance and leg-sweep.

c) Your opponent has a knife and seizes your lapel. Attack the knife-wielding hand with wrist-turn.

d) Your opponent has a knife. Use your coat to whip across his face and then snap-kick him in the groin.

B: *You Have A Baton*

a) Your opponent has a knife. Strike his wrist with the baton, then snap-kick at his groin and apply arm-entangle.

b) Your opponent is unarmed and swings at your face. Use both arms to block, then strike him with the baton and use it to apply arm-entangle.

c) Your opponent is unarmed and attacks you with a kick. Bar the baton across his shin and then drive it into his chest or throat, using a double-hand grasp throughout.

C: *You Have A Staff*

a) Your opponent is unarmed and advances to strike you. Crack him across the leg, then jab the staff into his ribs and apply arm-entangle.

b) Your opponent is unarmed and grabs the end of it. Snap-kick him in the groin and then twist the staff out of his hands.

c) Your opponent is unarmed and swings a punch at you. Crack the staff across his punching arm, then across his ribs. Seize his wrist and lever down with the staff against his elbow.

Section 6: Free Practice

Spend at least five minutes in a free-sparring situation with your partner. He will determine the format of attack without warning you first and you must respond quickly and effectively.

Section 7: The Cool-down

Undertake a full cool-down programme consisting of whole-body exercises of diminishing effort. Conclude with gentle static stretches.

21 Acknowledgements

The authors of this book gratefully acknowledge the contributions made by the following to this book:

Robert Clark for his valued analysis of self defence technique and his very real contribution to some of the techniques referred to in this book.

Edwin Stratton for the time he so willingly gave to discuss ideas and concepts of advanced self defence.

Tommy Morris for some valuable critiques of self defence situations and responses.

The police self defence coaches of Britain (excluding the Metropolitan Force) who have assisted Brian Eustace in the fine tuning of some of the technique sequences.

The Martial Arts Commission for providing an open forum for martial artists of different disciplines to meet and discuss in an atmosphere of development and cooperation.

Doctor James Canney for permission to refer to some of his findings in the field of martial art and self defence related injuries.

Jason Eustace for his willingness to be hurled around the family garden in the search for logical association of techniques.

Brian Eustace
David Mitchell

July 1987.

22 Further Reading

If you enjoyed reading this book we recommend you also read the following:

Self Defence in Action by Robert Clark (Stanley Paul, 1987).

The Official Self Defence Handbook by David Mitchell (Pelham, 1985).

Be Safe by Paula Mitchell and Brian Eustace (Macdonald, 1987).

index

Index